THE LAND
BESIDE THE
CELTIC SEA

THE LAND BESIDE THE CELTIC SEA

Some aspects of ancient, Medieval and Victorian Cornwall

by
Richard Pearse

TRURAN

Published by Dyllansow Truran.
Trewolsta, Trewirgie, Redruth, Cornwall.

© 1983 R. Pearse

Printed in Great Britain

ISBN PB 0 907 566 480
ISBN HB 0 907 566 499

CONTENTS

THE LAND BESIDE THE
CELTIC SEA

ILLUSTRATIONS

AUTHOR'S NOTE

These brief essays are intended to reflect something of the essence of Cornwall's past. A few of them attempt to go back to origins. The ancient inscribed stones, the Christian crosses (nearly all of them cut from tough hard granite), the astonishing medieval trade in tin, the sea fisheries, the ancient duchy, the pilchard, and china clay were some of the foundations on which the living Cornwall was built. These things are fundamental components of a past about which we still do not know enough.

Curiosity, but certainly not scholarship, prompted me to compile these chapters. Some of them, particularly those on inscribed stones, crosses and holiday resorts, give us only a mere glimpse of quite vast subjects, but they might still provoke some discussion or invite disagreement with the little that I have written. If so, all the better. Several chapters are about subjects that need no introduction; they have been investigated and written about over and over again. I make no apology for failing to add anything to our existing knowledge. But the great revival of interest in the past that we are now witnessing, whether it be as remote as the age of the saints or as near as that of the holiday resorts, is an opportune reminder that there is still much to be discovered and explained. Hence my brief incursion into a few aspects of our immensely rich past. It merits our attention.

I have included the chapters on James Silk Buckingham and William Pease because these two Cornishmen deserve to be better known. Their moral integrity, their intellectual stature and their achievements in their respective fields of activity put them head and shoulders above their fellows. They contributed in a modest degree to moulding and shaping the period in which they exercised their powerful intellects and on which they left their mark.

The essays on Restormel Castle, the holiday resorts and the diarist William Pease were first published in the Western Morning News, Plymouth, and are reproduced here by courtesy of the editor. The chapters on the sea fisheries, Cornwall's ancient capital, and the medieval tin trade have been adapted from articles from my pen that likewise appeared in that newspaper.

I am also indebted to Mr. H.L. Douch, curator for the Royal Institution of Cornwall, Truro, for supplying the photograph for illustration no. 19 and to the owners of the Woolf-Greenham Collection for the photographs for illustrations nos. 1 - 6, 8 - 14 and 24. The editor of Devon and Cornwall Notes & Queries has generously allowed me to make use of the invaluable material on ancient Cornish crosses contributed regularly to that journal over a period of seventeen years from 1950 to 1966 by the late Surgeon-Capt. G.E. Ellis R.N.

The bibliography contains some of the more specialised works and material to which I have referred in compiling these chapters. There are, of course, other more general, more recent and well known works on Cornish saints,

1

Cornish crosses, the tin trade, archaeology, the Black Prince etc., as well as the standard parochial histories containing material relevant to the Cornish background and environment.

CORNWALL'S ANCIENT DOCUMENTS OF STONE

At the opening of the present century about forty ancient inscribed stones, inscribed crosses, cross shafts and cross bases, nearly all of them in granite, existed in Cornwall. And still exist. They are memorial or tomb stones, and most of them, except cross shafts sculptured with fine Celtic ornamentation, fall into the category defined as rude pillar stones. These resemble very crudely shaped and rough-surfaced columns or megaliths. Although the inscriptions have been identified and translated or transcribed by archaeologists and other scholars, most of them remain a mystery in so far as the names on the stones cannot be identified with or related to events, known people or any aspect of Cornish history.

It is generally accepted that the majority of these monuments have Christian religious associations and that they were hewn, cut and erected in the period of six hundred years between the departure of the Romans from Britain and the arrival of the Normans. But at least fourteen of these stones bear no trace of Christian symbolism or epigraphs such as are cut on stones erected as memorials to people who were known in their time to be Christians. These fourteen or so stones might therefore date from the Roman period, which ended about the year 410. They are in the pagan tradition.

Arthur G. Langdon, the archaeologist, deciphered many, but not all, of the inscriptions on the stones known to him. These were published in volume I of the Victoria County History of Cornwall in 1906. He described the stones in detail but did not relate them to definite periods or events. Two assumptions can be made: every stone commemorated a prominent person, and secondly it was probably hewn and erected in or near the district where the honoured individual lived or was active. Such heavy objects could not easily be dragged or otherwise transported about the hilly and roadless countryside.

The persons named on these monuments may have been pagan or Christian tribal chieftains (often called kings), Celtic monastic 'bishops' or other notables (if indeed there were any). We can have a look at just a few of these stones, but we are still lacking the archaeological or other types of evidence that might tell us something about the people who are named on them. It should however be noted that the inscriptions on most of the monuments are so weather-worn as to be only partially legible. Hence the interpretations attributed to Langdon and to other archaeologists whom he quotes many not be acceptable to other authorities. However, they can be a basis for further discussion or investigation. The stones can be classified in a number of ways, one of which is given below:

14 bearing no form of Christian symbolism

9   bearing a simple Christian epigraph
5   bearing the Chi-Rho ( ) monogram, the earliest graphic
     Christian symbol
1   bearing the cross of St Anthony
13   including shafts of crosses bearing the cross as a symbol of
     Christianity.

These last thirteen stones are probably of later date than the others. The cross was adopted as a symbol of the Christian religion only at the beginning of the sixth century, when it replaced the Chi-Rho monogram.

The sketch map, page   shows approximately the distribution in Cornwall of the stones in the above list. Elsewhere in the British Isles such memorials occur mainly in Devon, the immediate Bristol Channel region, Wales, Cumberland and western Scotland. They also occur in Ireland. In these countries and districts bordering the Irish Sea Celtic Christianity took root and survived, preventing the infiltration of Anglo-Saxon paganism. Inscribed stones of Celtic i.e. Christian type have not been found in those parts of England occupied by the Saxon invaders in the two centuries following the collapse of Roman rule. It will be seen that the inscribed stones without Christian symbolism occur more frequently in the western than in the eastern half of the county.

There is, so far, no conclusive evidence that Christianity had been established in Cornwall during the Roman occupation of Britain. Some of the monuments bearing no Christian epigraphs were possibly erected in the transition period of the fifth century when Celtic Christianity was just beginning to replace paganism in Cornwall. Many years may have elapsed before any knowledge of Christian symbolism and epigraphy reached Cornwall from the eastern Mediterranean. Therefore a few Roman-type memorials of pagan appearance may have been erected to commemorate early Christian converts. The earliest Christian epigraphy appeared with the words 'hic jacit' ('Here lies' or 'here he lies'). In a few cases the stone also gives the immediate male parentage of the deceased person. This was a continuation of a normal Roman practice.

All the rude pillar stones found in Cornwall are very roughly hewn when compared with the better workmanship of Roman memorial stones elsewhere in England. Either the granite was too tough to give an inscription with a good finish, or the stone-cutters were not habitual craftsmen. The few Roman milestones discovered in Cornwall have no better finish than the non-Roman inscribed stones.

It is widely accepted that Christianity was introduced into the western part of Dumnonia (which comprised mainly what are now Devon and Cornwall) by missionaries or 'saints' from Ireland and Wales. Inscribed stones of Christian type must therefore have been erected not earlier than the beginning of the so-called Age of the Saints in the fifth

4

century. We therefore look for a direct connection between the saints and the Christian inscribed stones. Yet we find nothing definite to connect them, although the monuments at St Endellion, Southill and Fowey suggest there might be some connection.

Although these roughly shaped monuments were greatly venerated in the Dark Ages and the very early Middle Ages, nearly half of them have subsequently suffered misuse both by ecclesiastics and the public. They have been discovered built into the walls and foundations of churches, and used as foot-bridges across small streams. One was found propping up a barn roof, and another had had two holes pierced in the granite to fix the hinges of a farm gate. Some of the stones have been discovered in the past hundred and fifty years, and more may yet come to light.

The inscribed stone found in the wall of an old farm building at Rialton in St Columb Minor parish might be one of the oldest in Cornwall, and prove to be of unusual interest. It has no Christian symbolism. Rialton is close to ancient tin streamworks and only two miles from Carnanton in St Mawgan-in-Pydar where a large block of refined tin was found on the site of an ancient tin-smelting works, called a Jew's House. This block, now preserved in the County Museum at Truro, bears what can only be the official Roman stamp. It was therefore produced under Roman supervision or control. In another streamwork, situated between Rialton and Carnanton, brooches, coins, a tin vessel and bronze celts have been found. Apart from the coins, whose origin was not determined, these things date from the Iron Age. Then again a coin of Alexander Severus (A.D. 222-235) has been found at Pentire Point East, just four miles to the west of Rialton and overlooking the Gannel estuary lying just to the west of Newquay. It was in this third century that the Romans first began to show interest in Cornish tin. One Roman coin doesn't prove much - only in fact that someone brought it there - but is possibly another pointer to a Roman presence in the nearby Rialton district.[1]

This Rialton stone bears the inscription BONEMIMORI ILLI TRIBUNI in Roman capitals. A tribunus was either a Roman military officer or a government official. Since tin was virtually a Roman government monopoly the presence of an official in the district to supervise and assay the production of the metal would be quite normal. The available evidence suggests the possibility of tin production in the Iron Age continuing into, or resumed in, the third century A.D.

In the parish of Lewannick close to Launceston and the Devon border there were discovered in 1892 and 1894 two of the few monuments in Cornwall known to bear inscriptions in the Irish ogham system of writing. The inscriptions are also in Roman capitals. One of the stones carries the Latin inscription in horizontal lines in the Roman tradition, indicating that it could be older than the other. It is also without Christian symbolism, whereas the other stone - or rather a large broken section of a

5

stone - is inscribed vertically with '.. C IACIT ULCAGNI'. This makes it a Christian memorial; the words on the missing section would have included the name of the son of Ulcagnus.[2]

Irish incursions, raids and settlement in the western coastal districts of Britain took place intermittently during the two centuries immediately preceding the Roman withdrawal from Britain which began about the year 410. Ireland was not yet converted to Christianity. The older Lewannick stone could belong to this pre-Christian period of Irish settlement. Irish ogham stones were also found nearby in north-west Devon.

There was further Irish settlement in some western coastal districts after Ireland had been evangelised following Patrick's visit to that country in the year 432. The second Lewannick stone - or the discovered section of it - could well be of this period. It does not seem possible, so far, to relate this stone to the Irish missionaries who are said to have evangelised the extreme south-west parts of Cornwall in the second half of the fifth century, and the early sixth. Lewannick church is named after Martin, a saint in the Roman calendar, whereas if the district had been the abode or territory of an Irish missionary we would expect the patron saint to be that person.

It may or may not be a coincidence that an inscribed stone bearing no Christian symbolism, discovered at St Breock, near Wadebridge, carries the words ULCAGNI FILI SEVERI ((the stone) of Ulcagnus the son of Severus). This monument has the inscription in Roman capitals and could be a memorial to a pagan. Or it could be a Christian memorial erected before knowledge of Christian-style epigraphy had reached Cornwall. There seems to be no evidence of evangelisation by Irish missionaries in the Wadebridge district, whilst the parish church at St Breock is named after the Welsh missionary Brioc. Thus we do not know whether the Lewannick Ulcagnus is the same person as he who is named on the St Breock stone. The name Severus itself is of course Roman, suggesting Roman influence even if the person himself was not Roman.

What may be the oldest Christian stone in Cornwall was found at St Erth, the inscription reading (in translation) 'Here in peace rests...... Cunaide here in the grave he lies he lived XXXIII years.' The Latin inscription in Roman capitals occupies eleven very short horizontal lines across the face of the stone. One line is illegible through weathering. Two Roman features are the horizontal inscription and the age of the commemorated individual. Who was he? It is most unlikely that he was the Cunedda whose tribe are reputed to have driven pagan Irish invaders from North Wales in the first quarter of the fifth century.

The first graphic symbolism representing the Christian religion originated in the Near East in the third century. The Chi—Rho monogram ( ) is derived from XP, the Greek version of the first two letters of the name Christ. It was adopted by Constantine the Great early in the fourth century. There is a legend that it appeared on his battle standard in the year 317 when his troops invaded Italy from Gaul to liberate Rome from the pagan rule of Emperor Maxentius. The monogram was in use in Romanised Gaul about the year 350. At the end of the fifth century another symbol replaced it : the Greek cross in which all four limbs are of equal length and width.

In Langdon's time at the beginning of the present century no more than a dozen ancient stones bearing the Chi-Rho monogram had been found in Britain : five in England (all of them in Cornwall) and the others shared between Wales, south-west Scotland and the Isle of Man. Here again is evidence of Christianity and its symbols reaching the Celtic western fringe of Britain. Knowledge of the symbol reached Britain from the Eastern Mediterranean very probably by the route via south-west Gaul, when the rest of Britain was labouring under the pagan Anglo-Saxon invaders.

Possibly the earliest known occurrence of this symbol in Cornwall was on an inscribed stone discovered at Southill near the Devon border in 1891. The two names on the stone have no known connection with the district. Apart from the symbol the stone is of pagan type. The inscription reads 'CUMREGNI FILI MAUCI' ((the stone) of Cumregnus the son of Maucus). He was probably a petty chieftain.

Southill church is named after Samson, one of the more prominent of the Welsh missionaries, who spent much of his life in Brittany and died there about the middle of the sixth century. He is also patron saint of St Sampson's church at Golant, near Fowey. Only a mile and a half away from Southill is Linkinhorne, whose patron saint is the Breton Melor. That the Chi-Rho symbol occurs in a district where two neighbouring churches are named after saints closely connected with Brittany suggests that its presence there was due to direct contact with south-west Gaul, through which passed the permanent route from the eastern Mediterranean to the western fringe of Britain.

Contact between Southill and Armorica (now Brittany) probably began in the period from 450 to 470 when the first big migration of thousands of Britons, fleeing before the Saxon invaders, took place. These refugees fled westwards into Devon and Cornwall, whence they crossed the sea to Armorica. Another massive migration of Britons followed about a century later. So many of them poured into Armorica in these two large migrations - and there may have been others - that the territory acquired its new name of Brittany, the land of the Britons. Many Celtic missionaries, mainly from Wales and Ireland, followed the British emigrants in order to convert them to the Christian religion.

The only other Chi-Rho stone in East Cornwall is close to the north coast at St Endellion. It is, more precisely, a rude cross shaft. There is a suggestion of Anglo-Saxon in the lettering of the inscription, and this

7

could date it to the seventh century. The inscription is surmounted by an unusual representation of the Chi-Rho symbol in that three arms of the letter X seem to resemble the limbs of the potence cross. A simple Greek cross occurs on the reverse face.

This St Endellion monument is a memorial to one Brocagnus whom some writers interpret as a version of Brychan, a fifth-century petty king who held territory in South Wales, and some of whose many sons and daughters, according to legend, were missionaries in North Cornwall. The patrons of several churches in the region are said to be his offspring. In translation the inscription reads '(the stone of) Brocagnus here he lies the son of Nadottus.' St Endellion church is named after a woman missionary, Endelienta, one of Brychan's legendary daughters.

The three inscribed stones in Cardinham parish are without Christian symbolism, but this does not necessarily mean that all three must be memorials to pagans. One of them commemorates Vailathus, son of Vrochanus (or Brochanus?). Could he possibly be a member of the Brychan tribe? The patron saint of Cardinham is Mewbred, supposedly a Welsh woman missionary, and possibly a member of the same Brychan clan.

St Just-in-Penwith, the most westerly parish in England, has two rude pillar stones, one of them bearing the Chi-Rho monogram on its front face and the inscription running down a lateral side. The other has the inscription on the front, and a simple Greek cross incised on one of the lateral sides. Both stones are probably amongst the oldest yet found in Cornwall.

The best known inscribed stone is the so-called Tristan monument, now standing by the roadside about a mile north of Fowey. Many scholars believe that the commemorated Tristan is in fact the male partner in the Tristan and Iseult romance. He is described on the monument - a very roughly hewn slab of granite - as the son of Cunomorus, a petty chieftain who supposedly held some territory in Cornwall and in Brittany. He is believed to have been a contemporary of Samson, patron of the nearby church at Golant. Samson founded a monastery at Dol, in Brittany. Dol became the see of one of the seven original Breton bishoprics, its patron saint being Samson. The cross of St Anthony is carved in relief on the reverse side of the Tristan stone.

Another very well known stone - more accurately the inscribed base of a cross - is the Doniert memorial near St Cleer. The Latin inscription in hiberno-saxon minuscules reads DONIERT ROGAVIT PRO ANIMA, certainly not a pagan epigraph. It can be dated to the ninth century. Doniert, according to legend, was one of Cornwall's chieftains or petty kings.

Like the Doniert stone, two other inscribed shafts of crosses in East Cornwall reflect the strong anglo-saxon religious influence which for a long time hardly penetrated the more central and western parts of the county.

One of the stones is the monument at Lanteglos-by-Camelford which bears the words in the anglo-saxon language. The other stone is at Tintagel. It was discovered in 1875 in use as a gate-post, for which purpose it had been chipped around the sides. Both the front and rear surfaces are covered with the many-worded inscription in anglo-saxon capitals. The upper part of both faces bears an incised cross with its four equal limbs greatly widened at the extremities.

The fact that the last three monuments described above exist in East Cornwall and that there are no known stones displaying strong anglo-saxon religious influence anywhere else in Cornwall seems to confirm the belief that the Anglo-Saxon Church did not follow the Celtic cult of erecting memorials to noted Christians.

THE CROSSES AND THE SAINTS

Cornwall is Britain's richest treasure house of ancient Christian crosses, of which more than five hundred are known to exist within the county. The great majority, cut in granite, date from pre-Norman times down to the late Middle Ages. On the crosses, as on Cornwall's ancient inscribed stones, much valuable research has been carried out by several archaeologists and historians, amongst them J.T. Blight and Arthur G. Langdon. Much more recently the late Surgeon-Capt. G.E. Ellis, O.B.E., R.N. recorded and described with meticulous detail nearly two hundred crosses, together with some shafts and bases separated from the vanished crosses they once supported, existing in the eastern half of the county. His work, published in more than fifty parts of Devon and Cornwall Notes & Queries from 1950 to 1966, is an exceptionally rich contribution to our knowledge of a subject in which much still remains to be done.

These present notes are based largely on the scholarly research carried out by Langdon, supplemented or modified by the work of Ellis. They are intended to seek possible reasons for the way or method in which the two main types of Christian cross were distributed geographically in Cornwall.

The two main types are the Cornish wheel or round-headed cross, and the Latin cross. Many crosses have been discovered during the past hundred years or so, and it is likely that more of them will be unearthed, some of them quite literally so. There are still a few sites in the county without crosses where one might expect to find them. It is assumed that crosses remaining to be discovered will turn up in roughly the same ratio of Celtic wheel to Latin as those already known to us: three of the former to one of the latter.

In the two-thirds of the county lying to the east of an imaginary line drawn from Newquay to Truro there is an average of nearly one and a half crosses per parish. In the remaining western third the average is nearly two and a half. The evidence suggests there might, or perhaps should be, a connection between the Celtic missionaries or saints who are reputed to have brought Christianity to Cornwall, and the distribution or incidence of the two types of cross. The Cornish Celtic cult of erecting crosses came in after the age of the saints had passed, probably 150 to 200 years later, although there is no sharp dividing line for events that have left little evidence. The legends and reputation of the saints must have had a strong influence on this cult.

There are numerous minor variations of the Cornish wheel or round-headed cross. It is in fact the Greek cross, with its four limbs of equal length and width, sculptured in relief or incised, often on both the front and reverse faces of the circular head above the shaft. Some crosses are sculptured with fine Celtic ornamentation, but the majority are not. Others have architectural and stylistic variations, possibly due to the artistic fancy of the stone-cutters. A frequent variation is the so-called four-hole cross, wrongly named as such. This form of the Greek cross is no more than the simple cross fitting neatly into the wheel or ring encircling it. Purely for simplicity this Cornish Celtic wheel cross in its several variations will be referred to in this essay as the Greek cross. It was adapted from the simple cross when the ancient Celtic Church in Cornwall adopted this graphic symbol of Christianity. There may have been no specific reason for designing a ring or wheel to encircle the cross. It might just have happened without thought of any symbolic meaning. In the Latin cross the lower limb is much longer than the other three limbs. The cross can therefore not be fully encompassed within the framework of a wheel.

Since we are considering only the distribution of the crosses their variations will not be discussed. Nor will the medieval lantern cross, or crosses bearing on their shafts fine examples of Celtic sculptured interlacing and scroll patterns.

It is not known whether wooden crosses were used before crosses of stone came in. These latter were not hewn from the hard granite because they would look attractive. For the holy men who cut them or had them cut they had not only religious significance, but were put to practical uses. Many crosses served as wayside guide stones and landmarks on the exposed and roadless moors and along rough tracks and 'monks' ways' in difficult and wooded country. They were used as guide posts for people making pilgrimages to venerated sites that had been associated with saints. Others denoted resting points for bearers of coffins on their way to church. A few crosses with long shafts were set up by the wayside as praying or preaching points in the absence of a nearby church or chapel. Under Anglo-Saxon rule crosses were used as parish or manorial boundary posts. Elaborately ornamented crosses were erected in churchyards for devotional purposes. In our modern contemporary society ancient Christian crosses seem to have lost all meaning. Even in the Middle Ages and later some crosses have been used in the re-building or restoration of churches. This lack of reverence for the sanctity of Celtic religious relics may have been an expression of Norman dislike of the vanished Celtic Church.

Crosses are known to have been removed from their earliest site, but the majority are probably still in or very close to their original position. Road widening, new housing developments, mining and industrial growth, and exposure to possible damage are some of the reasons for shifting an ancient cross to a new site. Such positional changes are usually slight, so that the original general pattern of distribution is no doubt very much the same today.

It is convenient to examine the distribution of these ancient crosses by beginning in the extreme eastern region of the county. The following details do not pretend to be complete, but they provide a basis for further discussion.

In the 27 parishes running in an unbroken line down the border facing Devon from Morwenstow in the north to Rame in the south only 12 crosses have been recorded. And in the 23 parishes immediately behind and contiguous with these only 25 crosses have been noted. Thus we have these 50 parishes - nearly a quarter of the total in the county -sharing between them only 37 ancient crosses, far less than one twelfth of the known crosses in Cornwall.

It is significant that only a dozen of these 50 parishes have churches with Celtic saints as patrons. All the others have saints in other calendars i.e. Andrew, James, Olaf, Mary, Michael etc. As we move westwards to Bodmin Moor the crosses occur much more frequently. In the 16 parishes embracing parts of the Moor or bordering it 96 crosses have been recorded, an average of six each:

Parish	Patron Saint	Greek crosses	Latin crosses	Not identified/ damaged	Total
Advent	Celtic	1	-	-	1
Altarnun	Celtic	5	2	-	7
Blisland	Celtic	9	4	-	13
Bodmin	Celtic	5	-	2	7
Bolventor*	None	-	-	-	-
St Breward	Celtic	7	-	1	8
Cardinham	Celtic	6	2	-	8
St Cleer	English	3	4	-	7
St Clether	Celtic	6	-	-	6
Davidstow	Celtic	2	1	-	3
Lanteglos	Celtic	7	1	-	8
Linkinhorne	Celtic	1	-	2	3
St Neot	Saxon	1	8	1	10
North Hill	?	-	4	-	4
Temple	Roman	2	4	2	8
Warleggan	Roman	-	1	2	3
		55	31	10	96

We note here the prevalence of the Greek type of cross in parishes with Celtic patron saints: 49 Greek to 10 Latin; and the Latin type in parishes with patron saints in other calendars: 21 Latin to 6 Greek.

One of the above parishes - Blisland - originally had a Welsh patron saint, Adwenna, but in the Middle Ages she was exchanged for two saints in the Roman calendar. It was therefore an original Celtic foundation.

* Bolventor parish was formed in 1840 out of three contiguous parishes.

12

There has always been some doubt about St Neot's patron saint (as also of many other parishes). If it is true, as is sometimes thought, that St Neot has the same patron as St Neot in Huntingdonshire, then he was probably a Saxon, not a Celt. Hence eight of the ten ancient crosses within the parish are of the Latin type. We shall find that it is quite unique if any 'Celtic' parish in Cornwall were the custodian of eight Latin crosses and only one of its own Greek type.

The Greek cross was adopted as a graphic Christian symbol by the Celtic Church in Cornwall before the Latin cross became a symbol of the faith, and long before the christianised Anglo-Saxons finally conquered the whole of Cornwall early in the tenth century and set up their own bishopric. We find both types of cross in very many parishes including those with Celtic patrons, but in these the Latin cross would have been a later addition to the original Greek, probably after the monastic organisation of the Celtic Church was replaced by the diocesan system of the Anglo-Saxon Church.

If some parishes are now without a cross it does not mean that they have never had one. In over a thousand years, for relatively small things like crosses to get lost by theft, burial or misuse as building stone would not be abnormal. There are no means of finding out how many are missing.

The adoption of the Greek cross by the Celtic Church was made possible through communication with the Near East while the rest of England was still under the pagan influence of the Saxon invaders. There was uninterrupted communication through traders and religious men between the eastern Mediterranean and the lands, including Cornwall, bordering the Irish Sea via south-western Gaul as well as via the sea route around Portugal and Spain.

The Bodmin Moor region has a very much higher concentration of crosses than the extreme east and south-east of the county. There may have been a greater need of crosses in that exposed and deserted wasteland. But it is also likely that crosses in the districts nearest the River Tamar are thin on the ground because in their day the Celtic missionaries were thin on the ground in those parts. From the paucity of crosses it could be deduced that the Anglo-Saxon church did not make it a rule to follow the Celtic cult of erecting crosses.

Since the Welsh and Irish missionaries were the first to bring Christianity to Cornwall the tiny churches or oratories they set up must have been the earliest. Churches that were not Celtic foundations were probably built only after the installation of the Anglo-Saxon bishopric, although there was some Anglo-Saxon religious penetration into Cornwall before that.

We next have the region of the Welsh saints running down the north coast from Morwenstow to St Cubert, south-west of Newquay, with the contiguous inland parishes lying behind the coastal parishes. In these 37

13

parishes there have been recorded 65 crosses, distributed as follows:

48 in 20 parishes with Celtic patron saints
17 in 15 parishes with non-Celtic patron saints
0 in 2 parishes with unidentified patron saints

Again we find a much higher proportion of crosses in parishes with churches named after Celtic saints. And of the 48 crosses in these parishes 35 are of the Greek type, only 9 Latin and 4 undetermined owing to missing or damaged cross heads. There were of course no parishes as far back as the age of the saints: the word parish is used in this context since it is the easiest way of defining the approximate and assumed area of influence of a Celtic religious foundation or an active missionary.

The sketch map on page 79 shows the approximate situation of parishes with churches named after Welsh saints. Possibly a few less conspicuous missionaries have gone into oblivion and left no traces. It should be emphasised here that the life stories of nearly all the Welsh and Irish saints who evangelised Cornwall are wrapped in mystery, legend, doubt and Celtic lore. There is little authentic proof that this or that saint did all (if any) of the things that have been attributed to him or her, or that every church 'dedication' is the original or correct one. (Churches, some will say, are dedicated to God, never to human beings, be they saints or not). There are rare exceptions such as Samson and Petroc whose life stories were written before Norman times and have a ring of truth about them. Some medieval and subsequent writers have filled gaps in the biographies of saints and replaced missing facts and details with picturesque and imagined adventures, sometimes borrowed from legends about other saints, thus creating a tangle of confusing stories. Nevertheless, legends often have an origin based on a fact or a grain of truth. If they had not, they would not have survived. There is enough reliable evidence to confirm that groups of missionaries from Wales and Ireland did carry out some evangelising in Cornwall, although we do not know how much and for how long.

On 13 October in the year 1330 Bishop Grandisson of Exeter,[3] in a letter to the incumbents of all the churches in his diocese comprising Devon and Cornwall, reminded them that many of their churches, especially in Cornwall were dedicated to local and other saints whose names were not to be found in any religious calendar, and that the lives and legends of many of these saints were preserved in their churches. He therefore directed that two or three copies be made of such records before they were irreparably lost. In editing and publishing Bishop Grandisson's register in 1894 the Rev. F.C. Hingeston-Randolph reported that as far as he knew not one of these copies had survived. His comment implied that none of the originals still existed. Therefore we do not know today how much authentic fact was contained in the original records. Their loss has undoubtedly given rise to a great deal of unsubstantiated legend.

The Welsh missionaries are believed to have come to Cornwall in the period between 550 and 680, about a century later than their Irish predecessors. They travelled by sea (so we are told) and came ashore in what are now the Padstow and Newquay areas where a tidal estuary and a couple of inlets break into the long line of dangerous cliffs. Amongst the parishes in this 'Welsh' region there is no church named after an Irish saint, although opinions differ on this point. There are several parishes whose patrons, according to legend and shadowy tradition, were sons and daughters of Brychan, a South Wales chieftain. Although the Welsh tribal group or groups from which the saints emerged are said to have arrived over a period of some 130 years, legend asks us to accept that they were Brychan's children. This is of course parabolic language. They were members of his tribe, probably covering several generations.

If we think for a moment about the evangelisation of such a small territory as Cornwall it is difficult to accept the view that one hundred years separated the arrivals of the Irish and Welsh missionaries. Did the Irish come first, evangelise the extreme western parts of Cornwall, and then sit back and wait a hundred years for the Welsh to come and 'work' the rest of Cornwall with a little help from the Bretons?

There is apparently no obvious reason why both Irish and Welsh missionaries limited their christianising work. Cornwall was not then a separate region or known by that name. It was part of Dumnonia, comprising roughly the present area occupied by Devon and Cornwall. Tradition and legend leave the impression that Cornwall was over-run with Celtic missionaries. There may have been about a couple of dozen Irish and possibly some four dozen Welsh who were prominent enough to achieve lasting veneration or honest notoriety. At this distance in centuries it seems that it would not have required as many as six dozen missionaries to stamp out paganism in the county, but apparently it did. If the christianising lasted a long time - and it was possibly a slow process of radical penetration - then the work may have required a succession of missionaries over a few decades. Those who died might have been replaced by un-named new arrivals to carry on their work. But there is no parish with more than one Welsh or Irish patron saint.

If the names of parish patron saints mean anything to us then it is apparent that the missionaries did not convert the parts of Cornwall bordering the Tamar river. Yet the whole region was pagan and in need of conversion when the missionaries first came to Cornwall. Perhaps the holy men and women, inspired as they were by Egyptian monasticism, might have been passive sedentary people who by their meditation and withdrawal from the world thought they were setting an example of simple pure Christian living. Or again they may not have been welcome and were met with animosity or hostility in the districts close to the Tamar.

On the other hand it may have been the intention of many missionaries, perhaps of nearly all of them, to use Cornwall only as a stepping stone to the Continent. A lot of them did cross the channel to north-west Gaul, and several, both Irish and Welsh, bequeathed their names to places scattered about Armorica (now Brittany) as well as to places in Cornwall. The names of seven saints who had been associated with Cornwall were given to the cathedrals established in the seven original bishoprics in Brittany, a territory nearly eight times larger than Cornwall. The task of christianising Armorica was vastly greater than the work carried out in Cornwall. Some of the better known saints travelled back and forth between Cornwall and Brittany more than once. These two lands, inhabited by Celts having precisely the same origin and speaking in exactly the same tongue, must have been regarded as one country that was inconveniently divided in two by the channel.

Adjacent to Cubert, the last of the 'Welsh' parishes on the north coast, is Perranzabuloe, the first of a string of parishes running down the coast as far as Sennen, close to the Land's End, forming the northern part of the region lying to the west of Truro.

Again legend and tradition tell us that this region was very largely evangelised by Irish missionaries. They are believed to have come to Cornwall in groups or clans, each under a leader, in the second half of the fifth century and the early part of the sixth. Their landfall would have been St Ives Bay, the nearest accessible point on the coast to Ireland. Amongst the most notable of the leaders were Berriana, after whom St Buryan is named, and Ia, who gave her (or his) name to St Ives. There is also a sprinkling of Welsh saints' names in the region. Altogether in Langdon's time there were at least 188 crosses (probably some more not then recorded) spread over 82 parishes, apportioned as follows:

	No. of parishes	Greek crosses	Latin crosses	Unidentified crosses	Total crosses
Irish patron saints	18	45	1'4	2	61
Other Celtic patron saints	30	53	38	4	95
Non-Celtic & unknown patron saints	34*	14	16	2	32
	82	112	68	8	188

Once again we find a higher proportion of Greek crosses in those parishes with churches named after Celtic missionaries: 98 in 48 parishes, with 52 Latin crosses and 6 unidentified. The contrast is not so pronounced between Greek and Latin types as it is east of Truro.

Like Cornwall, Brittany was left to its own devices after the Roman withdrawal. In the ten years from 455 to 465, following the first Saxon invasion of Britain, Armorica received many thousands of British refugees fleeing before the invaders. A second wave of Celtic settlers from Britain crossed the channel towards the middle of the sixth century. Armorica then became known as Brittany, the land of the Britons. Many Irish, Welsh and British missionaries crossed to Brittany in the wake of the refugees, who were pagans in need of religion. It was perhaps normal that there was missionary activity on both sides of the channel, with both territories facing the same problems, and both of them open to the missionaries. Several parishes in the Falmouth and Mounts Bay districts have churches named after saints from Brittany, although a few of them may have originally come from Ireland or Wales. These two coastal districts were the easiest points of entry for people travelling from Brittany to Cornwall.

We now come to a significant variation of both the Greek and Latin crosses that is almost completely confined to the region lying to the west of Truro. On one face of the round-headed Celtic cross occurs a simple Greek cross, and on the other is depicted the figure of Christ with arms outstretched as if nailed to a cross. This new Christian symbol representing the Crucifixion was introduced following a decision made by a Council at Constantinople in the year 683. In Langdon's time 49 of these crosses were identified in 25 parishes to the west of Truro, but only four in three parishes east of Truro. About two-thirds of these 53 monuments are of the Greek type. The remainder are a similar variation of the Latin cross.

It is likely that knowledge of this new graphic symbol of Christianity reached Cornwall not later than the year 700 or thereabouts, while the region was still independent of Saxon rule, although we have no evidence as to when the cross was first introduced in the region. But why does it not occur generally throughout the county? Why is it confined to west Cornwall almost exclusively? And what was happening east of Truro (which did not then exist) to cause these crucifixion crosses to be excluded?

South-east Cornwall always remained outside the region of influence of the Celtic missionaries, and did not adhere to the Celtic Church. It eventually came under the influence of the converted Anglo-Saxons. When St Germans became the see of the first Cornish Anglo-Saxon bishopric early in the tenth century its power and influence was strongest in south-east Cornwall. In this district of 27 parishes close to the Devon border only 38 crosses have been recorded. Of these, 31 are Latin and only 7 Greek. St Germans parish itself has four of the former and none of the latter.

This south-east region, and the strip running down the long Devon border, are the only districts in which the number of Latin crosses exceeds the number of Greek crosses. They are also the only districts in which the patron saints in non-Celtic calendars are far more numerous than those in the Celtic calendar.

We have seen that:
1) the great majority of the large group of churches named after Welsh

saints are in that part of Cornwall geographically nearest to Wales.

2) most of the group of churches named after Irish saints are in that part of Cornwall closest to Ireland.

3) the group of churches named after Breton saints are nearly all in parishes geographically nearest to Brittany.

4) the district with the majority of churches not named after Celtic saints is geographically the furthest from Wales and Ireland, and also is not the nearest to Brittany.

It can hardly have been a coincidence that the distribution of the saints' names amongst the churches and parishes has resulted in this general yet very distinct pattern.

It is also unlikely to be a coincidence that the distribution of the two main types of cross followed the same pattern as the names of the saints, although it took place much later, the Greek type being far more numerous in the "Celtic" parishes and the Latin type in the non-Celtic parishes.

The distribution of Greek crosses seems to have been a deliberate policy or at least a custom, but of Latin crosses not. There was a time when only Greek crosses existed; the Latin cross seems to have come in with the Anglo-Saxon bishopric in Cornwall.

There does seem to be a definite after-relationship between the saints and the Greek crosses. The distribution of the latter is a fact, a true event in the history of Cornwall, even if it was a slow process. Yet the names, country of origin and places of temporary or permanent residence of the missionaries or saints are so closely wrapped in legend that they cannot be accepted as historical facts. Some of the legends about these holy men and women may well be true to fact, but literary and legendary evidence are, unlike the stone crosses, not archaeological evidence. Canon Doble's great work on the Celtic saints probably comes as near to historical fact as it has so far been possible to get.

If no Irish or Welsh missionaries had come to Cornwall to preach and teach Christianity the region would have accepted Saxon rule much earlier than it was eventually forced to, and it would not have adopted the Greek cross of the eastern Church. There would have been no saints to commemorate.

Where they stand the Greek crosses undoubtedly testify to the former presence of missionaries. The original site of a Greek cross probably signifies that a missionary lived or worked in the vicinity. The crosses were a form of memorial that were put to a useful purpose as guide, praying, preaching or boundary stones. As a religious legacy they would not have been erected just anywhere at random, but in many cases at venerated points or along tracks intimately associated with the honoured missionary. It was no problem in the eighth, ninth or tenth century, long after the age of the saints, to find out which districts or places had been regarded as sanctified by missionaries, of whom some were subsequently to become saints. Religious customs and knowledge about missionaries were transmitted down the generations like tribal traditions.

The small buildings, whether of wood or stone, used as Celtic oratories or churches, have not, apart from one exception, survived, and the sole survivor is a ruin. They have been knocked down or just crumbled away. But the granite crosses, being indestructible, have survived, although others may still lie hidden. As a collection they may, after further research, yet prove to be valuable archaeological evidence about Celtic Christianity in the Dark Ages.

THE GOLDEN AGE FOR CORNWALL'S TIN

The revival in the production of tin in Cornwall is a reminder that this industry is the oldest commercial enterprise in the Westcountry. Both Devon and Cornwall can look back on a long history of tin mining, but less well known is the international medieval trade in this metal, as well as the very extensive range of products in which it found an application. Tin was formerly an important article of trade and held a permanent leading place amongst England's exports. For several hundred years Cornwall and to a lesser extent Devon were the principal, at times the only, sources of supply of this metal for all those parts of the world known and open to European commerce.

Tin has been produced in Cornwall more or less continuously, but with varying fortunes, since pre-Roman times, possibly as far back as 1100 B.C. when the Phoenicians in their search for metals established a trading outpost at a place now called Cadiz. This continuous production implies a never ending demand for this metal which was normally used in alloy with one or more other refined metals.

The Roman occupation of Britain and Gaul created an important metal-working industry at Cologne and in the valley of the Meuse in the south of Belgium.[4] Here the towns of Huy, Namur, Liège and Dinant manufactured arms, shields, implements and tools of metal for the use of the Roman legionaries stationed at the garrison towns on the left bank of the Rhine - Speyer, Worms, Mainz and Cologne. During the first two centuries of the Roman occupation of Britain the tin for this metal-working industry was obtained from Spain, but when supplies from that source became less plentiful at the middle of the third century A.D. the Romans turned to Cornwall, which already had a tradition of tin production.

The Roman presence on the Rhine stimulated trade on three navigable water-ways - the Rhine itself, the Moselle, and the Meuse: The products of the metal-working centres included brooches, fibulae, buckles, enamelled jewellery, badges and so on, which were exported to distant parts of Europe.

Commerce slowed down when the Romans withdrew and the Merovingian Franks invaded Gaul, but a revival came in the seventh century when trade was renewed between England, now firmly under the rule of the Saxon invaders and settlers, and the Continent. The metal industry in the Meuse valley survived and then became important once more. Then early in the ninth century the Norman raids on north European and French Biscay coasts disorganised commerce, but in the tenth century it picked up again. Then came the first Crusades to the Holy Land, awakening the whole of western and central Europe and bringing about a great increase in economic activity and commerce.

Tin-plating, a process which the ancient Gauls brought with them from Asia, was a common and very general use for tin in France in the Merovingian period. Tin-plated articles in everyday use in the fifth and sixth centuries included sandal and belt buckles, brooches, bracelets, iron attachments or fittings for chests and caskets, spurs, mirrors, dishes, vases, bronze coins, saucers, spoons, badges, mordants for belts, clasps and so on. Many of these articles were of bronze, and already included a good percentage of tin before the coating of tin-plate was applied.[5]

Under Charlemagne who died in 814 still more uses were found for tin. An increasingly important application was in bell metal for bell-founding, established in England as well as on the Continent, although the larger and heavier types of cathedral and church bells came in later. In this Carolingian period tin was also used in the roofs of basilicas and churches, whilst in Italy and Spain ornamental bronze doors incorporating tin were manufactured for cathedrals. Early in the ninth century tin chalices, burettes, patens, candlesticks and ewers for monasteries and churches were in general use, although tin chalices were frowned upon and were officially sanctioned for use only in poor churches.[6]

In the tenth and eleventh centuries vessels of tin were being commonly used in monasteries: basins for cleaning table and cooking utensils, porringers, wine amphorae, bowls and pails, and vessels for washing chalices. Pewter ware for use in the refectory were introduced a little later. Many monasteries made their own pewter ware.

It is very evident that tin was in continuous demand all through the Dark Ages, but there is no evidence to demonstrate that supplies used on the Continent came from anywhere but England. The few deposits scattered about Europe are not known to have been active during the 600 years following the collapse of the Roman Empire. The important metal-working industry in the south of Belgium continued to obtain its supplies in London as soon as settled government had been established by the Saxons. This implies coastwise shipments from independent but unsettled Cornwall to Saxon England.

There is no written documentary evidence on the Cornish tin mining industry and its commerce before the twelfth century. Only after the accession of Henry II in 1154 were records kept, sparing at first, then more abundant. From then on we can watch the growth of the industry and build up the pattern of distribution and exports.

The Crown derived great profit from its almost monopolistic control of the refining and marketing of the metal, which made a very significant contribution to its revenues. In addition to the coinage or assay duty it had the first option on the purchase of any quantity up to the total output for re-sale at a profit through its appointed merchants or agents. Richard Coeur de Lion was probably the first of several monarchs to take up this option, and he did so on three occasions in the 1190's. It was done by way of loans advanced to him by Italian bankers against the security of future production of tin of corresponding value.[7] In the fourteenth century Edward II and Edward III were often desperately in need of cash. In the period 1313 to 1316 the industry came under the virtual control of the Italian Bardi Society to which Edward II was heavily in debt.[8] In 1347/8 a Hanseatic merchant was so hard pressed to buy up and ship tin across to Flanders to finance the Black Prince's military campaign against the French that his task was made less difficult by his appointment as Receiver of the Duchy.[9]

The marketing of tin produced in Devon and Cornwall in the Middle Ages was normally organised by London or foreign merchants, whether they purchased it freely from the tinners and dealers or were compelled to acquire it from the Crown's agent after pre-emption. The tin was shipped to ports where the merchants had store houses. From these it was forwarded to further depots before it finally reached the metal-working centres where it was required.

In the twelfth and thirteenth centuries Bruges was the leading trading emporium in northern Europe and the most important market for tin on the Continent. The trading republics of Venice, Genoa and Florence; the Hanseatic merchants of Cologne, Hamburg, Lubeck and Visby, and the merchants of Spain and southern France all had their store houses and agents at Bruges. Their business was to sell products from their own territories or from the Near East in exchange for manufactured goods and raw materials from northern Europe and England. The Genoese and Florentines sent their purchases of tin overland to Lyons via the busy Champagne fair towns and then down the Rhone; the Venetians (as later did Genoa and Florence) sent their own big ships twice a year to northern Europe. The Hanse merchants sent their tin from store houses on the River Zwijn near Bruges to the Baltic lands (all barred to English shipping), to Russia, central and eastern Europe, and to the metal-working industries at Aachen, Cologne, Liège and Dinant.

In the thirteenth century much tin from England found its way to Marseilles by two routes: one overland from Bruges and down the Rhone; the other, more important, direct from Cornish ports to Bordeaux and from there via Toulouse and Narbonne. Marseilles itself had little use for tin other than to re-sell it at a profit. In June 1248 Louis IX set out from Aigues-Mortes in a big convoy to the Holy Land, on the opening of the Seventh Crusade. Preceding him in April and May two convoys of ships carrying merchandise left Marseilles for Acre. Charter parties and promissory notes giving details of the cargoes of these ships have survived.[10] Amongst the variety of merchandise recorded in detail are several consignments of tin, with the individual weights, values and owners of all the lots.

A great deal of tin passed through Marseilles in the thirteenth century to destinations all around the Mediterranean including Pisa, Rome, Naples, Messina, Majorca, Famagusta, Acre, Alexandria, Damietta, Tunis, Bougie, Ceuta and Valencia.[11]

If Marseilles was the principal French transit port in the Mediterranean for tin (as well as other commodities) the Italians went further afield.[12] The powerful Bardi Society of Florence had their own branches at Acre, Famagusta, Constantinople, and Ayas in Armenia. Genoese merchants had offices in Beirut, Constantinople, Ayas and Azov near the estuary of the Don in the south of Russia, as well as at Acre. The Venetians were at Alexandria, at Candia in Crete and at Adalia in Turkey. Ayas in Armenia (now Turkey) was the starting point of a trade route into the heart of Asia via Tabriz in Persia. Azov, far away on the northern shore of the Black Sea, was on the main trade route across Asia to China.

At all these places in the eastern Mediterranean and beyond it Cornish tin was a regular commodity, and of sufficient consequence to be recorded by Francisco Pegolotti, a leading figure in the Bardi Society, in his treatise on commercial and trading practice written in the first half of the fourteenth century. In it he compares the price in London of tin from Cornwall with its price in Bruges, Cyprus, Armenia and many other places around the Mediterranean. He gives notes on the currencies, weights and measures employed in the various countries, and states where or through which channels the different trading cities obtained their supplies of tin. His treatise deals with all manner of products, yet none, apart from wool, is mentioned so frequently as tin. And there is no suggestion that it came from anywhere but England. At all these trading places it was included in the list of customs tariffs and tolls on commodities that were regularly handled at their markets.[13]

One of the largest outlets for tin from the early thirteenth century down to the Reformation was the production of bell metal for casting cathedral and church bells. In England alone many thousands of such bells were manufactured before the Reformation, weighing anything from a hundred-weight or two to several tons each. Bell-founding was a specialised craft, and bell-founders of great repute existed in many medieval cities, notably London, York, Salisbury, Exeter, Bristol, Gloucester, Worcester, Lichfield, Norwich and King's Lynn.[14] The sharpness and tone of a bell depended not only on the proportion of tin incorporated in the metal, and in the thickness of the mixture to be cast, but also on the skill of the founder. The proportion varied generally between one part of tin to three parts of copper, and one of tin to five of copper.

Occasionally small quantities of tin were purchased by the Crown for use in construction work, in the founding of bells, or in other ways not specified. In the year 1245 Henry III had the fine Norman Abbey church of

23

St Peter at Westminster pulled down, although it was barely one hundred years old, in order to replace it with a church more worthy to serve as the shrine to Edward the Confessor. Construction on the new Abbey church began at once and took several years to complete. Two tons of tin from Devon in 1247 and another five tons from Cornwall in June 1252 were ordered for this work.[15]

In 1248 small amounts of tin and lead were delivered to Corfe Castle in Dorset. In 1252 two lots of tin were purchased for delivery to the constable of Dover Castle, one lot to re-cast three large bells for the church there, the other for a building job. In 1253 and 1254 three lots of tin and one of lead were required for delivery to Freymantel Park at Kingsclere, in Hampshire, where Henry III had a residence with a chapel. And in February 1262 a quantity of tin had to be delivered to Windsor Castle for use in building work.[16]

In England relatively little true pewter seems to have been made before the thirteenth century, but by about 1425 more tin was being used in pewter ware than in any other type of product with the possible exception of church bells. At first there were two types of pewter ware: the finer quality required brass to be blended with the tin, and for the lower grade the alloy was 26lb of lead with one cwt of tin. In 1438 the London Pewterers' Guild issued an ordinance stipulating the standard sizes of the full range of pewter dishes from large chargers weighing 7lb each down to small moulds and bowls of 1lb each, and small saucers weighing 4lb to a dozen.[17]

On the Continent, which in the Middle Ages relied almost entirely on supplies of Cornish tin, there was a revival in the manufacture of domestic articles, as well as new types of ware, made of tin and pewter, replacing vessels and utensils made of wood, clay or copper. Ewers, large and small water jugs, cruets, salts, mustard pots, ornamentation on belts and jewel caskets, tin-plating of bath tubs, large and small drinking pots, spoons, wine cups, vessels for serving wine, vases, chandeliers (only in Belgium), shaving dishes, trays and ink pots were some of the products in which tin was commonly used.[18]

A further stimulus to the production of tin in the Middle Ages was its use in the manufacture, usually by casting in moulds, of enormous quantities of pilgrims' badges and medallions.[19] These were sold to pilgrims at the holy places and shrines, much as cheap trinkets are now sold at Lourdes and to holiday crowds at modern seaside resorts. Tens of thousands of pilgrims a year made their way to such places as Canterbury, Walsingham, Rome, Mont St Michel, the Holy Land, Tours, Amiens, Chartres, Aix-la-Chapelle and several others, whilst over half a million pilgrims made their way every year to the shrine of St James the Apostle and Martyr at Santiago de Compostela in Spain. Badges were made for just about every saint in the calendar, each bearing an effigy supposedly representing the saint. The most popular saint was St Michael the Archangel.

Now that our ancient tin mining industry has acquired new life and is expanding its activities it is opportune to look back over the centuries and reflect how effectively it helped to sustain our medieval monarchs, and how metal-working industries all over Europe came to depend on it for their continuing existence. The story of the modern commerce in tin will never be as varied and as picturesque as its medieval history.

ORIGINS OF CORNWALL'S SEA FISHERIES

Cornwall probably has as long a tradition of sea fishing as any other British maritime county. There were two main types of commercial sea fishery: the larger fishes such as conger, hake, cod, pollock, ling etc., which were caught by hook and line; and the smaller fishes such as pilchards and mackerel, caught in nets. We do not know precisely when these types of fishery became established as commercial enterprises since no documentary records go back beyond the twelfth century, and from then on they are only fragmentary and often incidental. Only regular government participation in an industry by way of taxes or duties can ensure that one aspect or another of its factual history can be officially recorded in the national archives. We thus have to scratch around elsewhere for information on the early fisheries.

Much of the available material points to Bayonne, in the Basque country of south-west France, being closely involved in the Cornish fisheries. In the second half of the twelfth century a group of Bayonne merchants established close trading relations with Cornwall, buying appreciable quantities of tin which they shipped to Poitou, to other parts of south-west France, and to northern Spain.

Some time later, in 1202, the same merchants were granted by King John the exclusive right to purchase whales caught between St Michael's Mount and Dartmouth. Whales were frequently found in and near the Bay of Biscay, and were caught mainly by Basque whale hunters. A further concession granted to these merchants by King John gave them the exclusive right to buy, salt or cure hake and conger in Cornwall.[20]

This concession merely confirmed and regularised an existing state of affairs, since some thirty years earlier these cured fish were listed in the Bayonne custumal as being subject to import tolls. The custumal of the port of San Sebastian just across the border in Spain also included at the same period hake, conger and tin as dutiable imports.

The shipowners of Bayonne were no less enterprising than their fellow merchants. Early in the thirteenth century they formed a co-operative that gave them the monopoly of the carrying trade between the newly founded port of La Rochelle and their home port. La Rochelle was used as a transit depot for the distribution of merchandise from England, and the assembling of goods to be shipped to England. The Bayonne co-operative fixed the rates of freight which all members were compelled to charge. The rates included conger at eight sols per thousand, and hake at three deniers per thousand.[21]

When we realise that Bayonne was a staging point on what was possibly the busiest route used by medieval pilgrims proceeding to the shrine of St James the apostle and martyr at Santiago de Compostela in

The Woolf-Greenham Collection.

Inscribed stone, Rialton.

Inscribed Irish ogham stone, Lewannick church.

The Woolf-Greenham Collection.

Inscribed Irish ogham stone, Lewannick churchyard.

The Woolf-Greenham Collection.

Inscribed Chi-Rho stone, Southill.   *The Woolf-Greenham Collection.*

Inscribed stone with Greek cross, St. Endellion
The Woolf-Greenham Collection.

31

Inscribed stone, Welltown, Cardinham.   *The Woolf-Greenham Collection.*

32

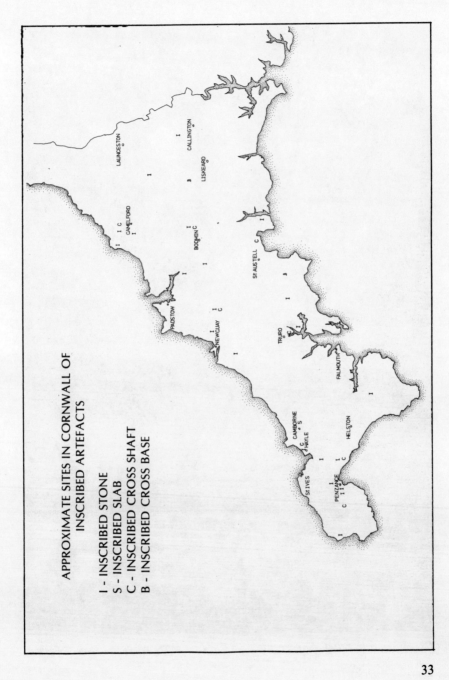

APPROXIMATE SITES IN CORNWALL OF
INSCRIBED ARTEFACTS

I - INSCRIBED STONE
S - INSCRIBED SLAB
C - INSCRIBED CROSS SHAFT
B - INSCRIBED CROSS BASE

33

Greek cross in relief, Sancreed.　　　　　*The Woolf-Greenham Collection.*

Incised Greek cross, St. Breward

The Woolf-Greenham Collection.

Crucifixion cross, Boskenna, St. Buryan. *The Woolf-Greenham Collection.*

Crucifixion cross (reverse side), Boskenna.
The Woolf-Greenham Collection.

37

Four-hole cross (with modern shaft), Carminow Cross, Bodmin.
The Woolf-Greenham Collection.

north-west Spain, we see the commercial importance of the town for its merchants. This most popular of the annual long distance religious pilgrimages was undertaken by rich and poor alike. The pilgrims came from Britain and most territories in western and central Europe, and are estimated to have numbered several hundred thousand every year. Quite a large percentage of these passed through Bayonne on both the outward and homeward journeys. Here, as at all staging places, the pilgrims had to be provided with shelter and food. Dried or cured fish would have been an important article of their diet.

In Cornwall in the fourteenth century the duchy havener regularly accounted for tolls or fines (fees) paid by merchants for the privilege of purchasing salted or dried fish for export. Never is the destination or quantity mentioned, and only occasionally the name of the merchant and the type of fish e.g. "6s 8d de fine Th. Taillo pro empcione dentricium" (hake).[22]

Sometimes, when export licences had to be obtained, as in 1364 following an interruption in exports, more details might be revealed e.g. "Licence to Wm Trevenugh to ship from Plymouth and Mousehole 30.000 dried hake to Gascony", or "Licence to Robt. Glemmoe and Nicholas Cardren of Market Jew (Marazion) to ship 100 tons of fish from Mousehole."

From time to time instructions were issued for the purveyance in Cornwall of fish for the Black Prince and his entourage: in 1358 and 1359 whiting had to be sent by sea from Cornwall to London and Sandwich respectively; in 1364 10.000 dried hake and 10.000 salted ling had to be purveyed in Cornwall and sent to Gascony. By medieval standards such single transactions were far from small; they would not be regarded as trifling even today. The figures indicate that sea fishing and fish curing must have employed a large number of fishing boats and professional fishermen.[23]

There seem to have been no exports by the Cornish fisheries in the thirteenth and fourteenth centuries to destinations other than in the Bay of Biscay. In the Norwegian and North Seas adequate quantities of cod, haddock and herring were caught for sale in northern countries and also for export to Gascony.

In the first half of the fifteenth century preserved hake, ling, pollock, cod, herring and seim (fish oil) were shipped from Cornish ports to Southampton,[24] apparently to be transhipped for export by Venetian and Genoese carracks, which in that period paid an annual trading visit to northern Europe, with Southampton as one of their two, or at the most three, ports of call.

The granting of a concession to Bayonne merchants in 1202 presupposes the existence of both fishing and fish-curing activities in Cornwall, certainly involving individuals but possibly not large scale organised groups. But let us go back to pre-Norman times to find out whether there could have been an organised fishing and curing industry. Cornwall was then often in a state of anarchy or non-government and plagued by Danish pirates seeking plunder. In the year 1050 the see of the Cornish bishopric at St Germans was withdrawn to Exeter; the official reason for this retreat was its continuing exposure to raids by pirates on the coasts.

The chronically unsettled conditions would at that time have made it impossible for any commercial fishery, involving continuous imports of salt and exports of worthwhile quantities of cured fish, to function anywhere on the Cornish coast or within its estuaries. There were no towns; and fishing villages as we know them did not exist. The coastal regions were too unsafe to inhabit.

Nor would there have been a local salt producing industry productive enough to provide sufficient sun-dried and wind-dried salt to maintain a commercial fishing industry.

The important pilchard fishery probably came into existence late in the eleventh or in the twelfth century after the risk of coastal raids had diminished. The use of seine nets for catching pilchards in shallow coastal waters continued without a break for centuries. Pilchards approached the coast in compact shoals and in quantities large enough to warrant the use of seine nets. They were caught, not in hundreds, but in tens of thousands at a time, far too many for immediate local consumption and too many for salting down for use by a small rural population in off seasons. Merchants and fishermen did not invest in boats, seine nets and large salt imports to be used just once a year. They would have made a few sorties during the pilchard season that might last from six to eight months. Obviously pilchards were caught for salting down for export as well as for local consumption.

Nothing is known about the size of early seine nets. In the immediate post-medieval period they might be from 600 to 900 feet long and from 40 to 60 feet wide or deep. When the shoal came close inshore the net was paid out in a wide arc to trap the fish between the net and the shore. When the two ends of the net were drawn together there was no escape since the net was weighted down to reach the sandy sea bed. The fish were caught without getting entangled in the meshes.

Seine nets were in use on the Cornish coast in the late thirteenth century, but they may have been introduced much earlier. The word 'seine' is derived from the Saxon word 'segne', and this suggests that this method of net fishing came to Cornwall with the Saxons. If the method had been invented by Cornish fishermen a Cornish or Celtic word would have been used to describe it. The word 'pilchard' is derived from the Celtic word 'pilseir', and occurs in medieval documents as 'pilcher.'

Pilchards have a high content of oil, known as 'train oil', a word derived from Low German meaning 'drip' or 'drop'. This train oil was both as a lamp fuel and as an ingredient in a sharp fish pickle. In the thirteenth century there was an establishment in the Fowey river designed for extracting oil by pressing the fish.[25] Much later oil was obtained during the salting process by pressure during bulking and after the fish had been packed between layers of salt in the hogsheads being made ready for export.

When we come to the fourteenth century we have a more comprehensive picture of the extent of Cornwall's commercial fisheries. There were five main centres of the industry: the Lostwithiel-Fowey region, including the adjacent coasts; the Falmouth district including St Mawes and the porths as far as the Lizard; Mounts Bay; St. Ives, and the group of porths on the north coast, including Porth Quin, Port Issac and Port Gaverne.

The Mounts Bay district was the most important, with fisheries at Mousehole, Newlyn, Penzance and Marazion-St Michael's Mount. Also associated with Mounts Bay were half a dozen small fishing ports along the coast between Mousehole and St Ives. Three weekly markets were held, one each at Mousehole, Penzance and Marazion in turn on Tuesdays, Wednesdays and Thursdays. Catches surplus to immediate local needs were sold to merchants for salting down or dry curing, both for storing and for export.

Customs returns provide information about imports of salt, an important aspect of the curing industry. Mousehole, Fowey, Lostwithiel and the Fal district were the main importing centres during the fourteenth century. Imports at Newlyn, Penzance, Marazion and St Ives were rare. It is likely that these places drew their supplies of salt normally ex-bond from storehouses at Mousehole, the chief importing port.

Salt for Cornwall's early fisheries came traditionally from Le Conquet and Guerande in South Brittany, and from Vermeu and San Sebastian in Spain. In the later Middle Ages and early Tudor period the main source was Bourgneuf, on the border of Brittany and Vendée. It was always described as 'Bay salt' in shipping documents, originating from the Bay of Bourgneuf. The Bayonne merchants who may well have been responsible for establishing the commercial fisheries in Cornwall on a permanent basis, would certainly have obtained their salt from San Sebastian or South Brittany, or both. It was an obvious advantage for them to have this two-way traffic: salt inwards to Cornwall, and cured fish and tin outwards. It was unnecessary for the Cornish fisheries to turn to Europe's largest source of mineralised salt in Poland.

Although documentary evidence on the early fisheries is patchy there is enough to confirm that they formed a significant part of Cornwall's economy, and provided continuous employment for the fishermen and fish curers, and for the boat builders who supplied the fishing craft. The fisheries probably benefited more people than the tin mining industry. Even in periods of famine the shortage of food could always be supplemented by fish, of which the sea contained great abundance. For centuries fish constituted the greater part of the diet of most of the population.

A CASTLE TO SERVE AN INDUSTRY

The significant thing about Restormel Castle is its ancient connection with an industry. Its construction in the form of an earthwork with timber attachments began at an unknown date, probably between 1070 and 1100. It was nothing more than an insignificant Norman baronial residence, built only because Norman barons normally built such things. It began to acquire some small notice in the second half of the twelfth century when the tin-mining industry was revived.

The castle looks down from a spur, some two hundred feet high, dominating the Fowey River at a slight bend just over a mile north of Lostwithiel. The chosen site was a good one since it provided a clear view up and down the valley for one and a half miles each way. Yet there was an equally good site at a higher altitude on the opposite bank of the river.

The administrative centre (if it could be called that) of the tin mining industry and the principal market for the sale of the refined metal was at Bodmin. Exports, whether to the Continent or to London, went by sea. The baronial Cardinan family to whom the castle had passed by marriage saw an opportunity to extend their influence and wealth by founding and fostering the growth of a suitable seaport for the shipment of the tin. They did this at a place now called Lostwithiel, and obtained for it the grant of borough status with the usual weekly market and yearly fair and the normal medieval privileges for its inhabitants. The new seaport borough on its tidal river was a valuable source of income for its landlord; all the shipping and market dues and tolls and the rent of every shop, cottage and garden plot in the place went to him.

The tin mining industry was virtually a royal monopoly which brought much revenue and profit to the Crown. From 1231 onwards its revenues went to Henry III's younger brother Richard, whom he appointed Earl of Cornwall. It could have come as no surprise to anyone that at last in 1268 Earl Richard acquired Restormel Castle and the borough of Lostwithiel on behalf of the Crown from the last member of the Cardinan line. He died soon afterwards in 1272. His son Edmund who followed him as earl carried out the plans for the further expansion of the industry and its profitable export trade. This was the real purpose behind the Crown's acquisition of the castle and borough.

Amidst the changes taking place Restormel Castle got its share of attention. The interior apartments surrounding the central courtyard were reconstructed in stone, with the addition of the chapel which was projected through the circular curtain. Whatever had previously existed inside the curtain was transformed into apartments on two floors equipped with a vast kitchen. Apartments or accommodation in stone were also built outside the moat on the west side, but these have since been demolished. It

43

was at this period - the last quarter of the thirteenth century - that the castle assumed its final form, which is clearly recognisable today.

The rebuilt structure, worthy of its new owner, was obviously planned as a prestige building. It was the great period of bastides and planted towns, and the Restormel-Lostwithiel complex had all the appearances of a bastide except that the castle was in no position to defend the town from attack on its vulnerable seaward side. It may possibly have been Earl Edmund's intention to take up permanent residence there himself, but as we shall see, he did not. At least the castle was a building worthy to be visited by foreign merchants or their factors who came in their ships to negotiate contracts for the purchase of tin. With the earldom exchequer, maritime administration, stannary control, justice and other earldom affairs now centred at Lostwithiel many visiting dignitaries would have to be received and entertained. It is unlikely that important visitors would have been allowed to go away without being invited to this show-place by whomever was in charge of it: the constable or keeper.

Earl Richard is known to have visited Cornwall at least five times, but there is no evidence that he ever came to Restormel. And for a good reason: it was not his property until he purchased it near the end of his life. It has been said that his son Edmund made it his permanent residence. But did he?

Much of Edmund's life from the moment he became earl in 1272 until he died in September 1300 was spent on national rather than earldom affairs, acting as regent for his cousin Edward I. Edward was absent on Crusade in the Holy Land when he succeeded to the throne in 1272. He returned home for his coronation in August 1275, and during those three years Edmund, surrounded by his advisers, was involved in running the Government of the country.[26]

In 1277 Edmund was himself absent in Wales on a military campaign. Then we find him acting as regent again in 1282, 1283 and 1284; yet again for three long years from May 1286 to August 1289, and once more in 1297 and 1298. He was certainly not able to remain in close touch with the machinery of government while sitting permanently in his castle overlooking the River Fowey. It is possible that he paid occasional visits to his earldom since he was continually busy raising funds from that source for the king's military expeditions, which succeeded one another through most of the reign. Much of this revenue came from the tax and the pre-emption profits on tin, from the many Cornish estates, from customs duties at the ports including the prisage of wine, and the profits of the judicial courts.

In 1337 when the earldom was raised to a duchy Prince Edward, later known as the Black Prince, became its first duke. It has been said that he too was a not infrequent visitor to Restormel, bringing displays of ceremonial pageantry. In fact he came only three times to the castle. He arrived there a few days before August 24, 1354, and left again between September 2 and 10. On this last date he was at Launceston on his way back to London. He did not come to Restormel again until 1362, when he spent Christmas there. The third visit can be deduced from an order signed by himself on board ship at Plymouth, when he was about to sail for Gascony. In this document he instructed that a sum of money should be paid to John de Kendale, Receiver of the Duchy, in reimbursement of expenses incurred on his behalf during his stay at Restormel between St Matthew's day (Feb 24) and Easter, 1363.

These three occasions seem to have been the only ones on which Restormel saw any ceremonial pageantry. Formerly as a baronial home it was insignificant, but it served its limited purpose. Then the Crown stepped in and took it over as a useful adjunct to its policy of increasing the state revenues from tin. At the bi-annual Lostwithiel markets tin was sold for export to every part of the known world at that time. If the walls of Restormel could speak we might hear stories of ships coming up the River Fowey with a variety of wares from such places as Bayonne, Bordeaux, Bruges, Lubeck, Narbonne, San Sebastian and Vianna; or voices making deals in tin. Such were Restormel's medieval associations, regular commerce and business rather than occasional pageantry and splendour.

CORNWALL'S ANCIENT CAPITAL

Thirty miles west of Plymouth on the A38 road through South Cornwall is Lostwithiel, too small and too quiet to be called a town, and too large to be treated as a village. Nevertheless it is an ancient royal borough, but is too modest to bask in its medieval glory. It lies on the floor of the valley of the River Fowey at the upper limit of tidal waters, six miles from the sea. The town has crept slowly up the gentle slope to the east and the much steeper hills to the west, merging into woods and sloping pastures. A mile or so both upstream and downstream the level valley bottom is no more than 200 to 400 yards wide.

Up the valley to the north the lateral slopes of conifer plantations and deciduous woods constitute some of the most pleasant riverine scenery in the west of England. Here the river, often hidden in the woods, gurgles and bubbles over rocks and boulders, sweeping past still pools under the lurching old trees growing out of its banks. Below the town where the valley broadens the tidal waters at flood times still penetrate the silted flats that are now at the stage of transition between marsh and pasture.

A stroll in the not very elegant streets will reveal a little architectural evidence that suggests something unusual about the place, giving it an atmosphere of faded dignity, age and maturity. Every village and country town has its venerable old church, but this one is just a little out of the ordinary. The lantern tower surmounted by a spire, the clerestory windows in the north and south walls and a disproportionately large east window are three architectural features that are rare in Cornwall. Not far away by the river are some large remnants, much restored and adapted for different uses, of a group of government stannary buildings erected between 1270 and 1300, with some of the original buttresses. They are the oldest non-ecclesiastical stone buildings in Cornwall, if one excludes castle ruins.

Then there is the fourteenth century packhorse bridge over the River Fowey. Its piers which support the five original arches now stand in a dozen feet of sand and rubble that have accumulated over the centuries. Next you have the undisturbed grid pattern of the few central streets and very narrow alleys, confirming that Lostwithiel is a planted town of Edward I's time,[27] although the original settlement dates from the latter half of the twelfth century.

The remains of the stannary buildings and the street grid lay-out are the only physical reminders, together with Restormel Castle a mile upstream, of Lostwithiel's medieval career as a centre of commercial, civil administrative, tin-smelting and shipping activities. Tinners, merchants and foreign seamen then mingled in its narrow streets.

Lostwithiel was probably the first settlement in Britain to have been created specifically to meet the transportation needs of an industry. This happened in the second half of the twelfth century when nearby Bodmin was the centre of the region that yielded and refined almost all the tin then produced in the county. As the nearest navigable point for sea-going ships Lostwithiel was created as a port to serve as Bodmin's gateway to the London and continental markets from which the much sought metal was distributed to the leading metal-working centres. The feudal lord of the manor obtained from the Crown about the year 1190 its first borough charter of liberties.

All through the thirteenth century the tin producing industry continued to flourish. Henry III's younger brother Richard, Earl of Cornwall, was granted all the profits of the stannaries from 1231 onwards. In 1257 his election as King of the Romans, with his coronation taking place at Aachen, misfired as a political move but it proved to be an economic advantage. Richard conferred trading privileges on some of his German cities and saw to it that several hundred Hanse and other European merchants got their share of the tin (and wool) they needed. After, of course, he had made his own profit.

In 1268 the Crown took the first step in re-organising the industry in order to exercise closer control over both tinners and merchants. Earl Richard puchased the borough of Lostwithiel and Restormel Castle from their owner, granting the town a new charter raising it from a seignorial to a royal borough and conferring upon it the right to have a Merchant Gild which, in effect, was the municipal governing body. During Richard's long tenancy of the earldom tin had become a still more significant factor in state finance and the third most valuable of the nation's exports. It was time to remove the principal market for the sale of the metal to Lostwithiel from Bodmin where the prior and his merchants had too much influence. It was most desirable that such an important market for a product that was virtually a state monopoly should be under the control of a royal rather than a monastic borough.

Earl Richard died in 1272 but his son Edmund who succeeded him as earl carried through the planned re-organisation. He ordered that Lostwithiel should be the sole staple of tin in Cornwall, and suppressed the other assaying centres and markets at Liskeard, Truro and Helston as well as Bodmin. Henceforward all the tin produced and refined in Cornwall had to be brought to Lostwithiel for assaying and coining prior to the bi-annual sales at its market. Edmund erected the stannary and earldom administrative buildings. They stood just back from the quay bordering the river, and rose like giants of stone above the narrow streets of small timber and cob cottages. The new buildings included the Shire Hall for the county court and assizes, the earldom exchequer, the Hall of the Stanners with its tin storage cellars, and the prison for tinners sent there by their own stannary courts. Lostwithiel was thus the capital of a county that was a virtual palatinate. It was during this last quarter of the thirteenth century that the original pattern of streets - if any - was swept away and replaced by the new plan that has since remained practically unchanged.

It was undoubtedly the intention of Edward I to make a bastide of Lostwithiel, but like so many similar projects attempted by this medieval town planner in England and France this one was destined within a century to become little more than a ghost town. The tin mining and smelting industry moved westwards to Truro and beyond, leaving Lostwithiel with nothing to replace it.

In 1337 when the Duchy of Cornwall was created to replace the old Earldom the borough had nearly 400 burgages, comprising a population at least as numerous as it is now. The period from 1200 to 1350 was Lostwithiel's golden age, the last 80 years from about 1270 having been the most active. For nearly 200 years trading vessels from as far as Portugal and the Low Countries rode up the river from Fowey on the incoming tides to exchange their cargoes of mixed merchandise for the goods Lostwithiel had to offer: tin, cheese, butter, corn and cured fish.

All this water-borne traffic into and out of Lostwithiel gradually came to an end by the beginning of the fifteenth century. Sand, gravel, rubble and mud from several tin streamworks up the valley to Bodmin Moor were carried down by the fast running river to meet with tidal water at the port of Lostwithiel. With these unwelcome deposits the depth of water there diminished progressively until sea-going vessels could no longer reach the quayside.

For a long time Lostwithiel was a chapelry within the large parish of Lanlivery. Like its mother church, the chapel came under the control of a Benedictine priory situated five miles away, which itself owed allegiance to the Benedictine Abbey of St Sergius at Angers, in France. The chapel was enlarged in the thirteenth and fourteenth centuries when first the tower and then the spire were added. After the creation of the Duchy in the fourteenth century the borough's feudal lord was Prince Edward of Wales, heir to the throne and known to history as the Black Prince. Frequently visited by foreign merchants and Duchy of Cornwall dignitaries, but only three times by the prince himself with his retinue of knights, Lostwithiel was now endowed with a parish church worthy of its status. The octagonal tower surmounted by the slender spire with lights at the four points of the compass, and the high clerestory windows - very unusual in such a small church in Cornwall - indicate French influence, probably due to the Angers connection.

Little of architectural interest has appeared and survived in the streets since the Middle Ages. The lack of any growth in population during eight centuries has always completely stultified new building development. The town became a backwater in the fifteenth century. And it remains a backwater, and this today is probably an advantage. No one knows when the cob dwellings of the medieval town were replaced, for no obvious timbered Tudor houses have survived. A few Georgian houses and cottages fill the gaps amongst Victorian dwellings, whilst an attractive group of three large attached late Georgian or early Victorian houses facing the north side of the church add something to the area in which they stand. The only other building of note is the Guildhall, erected in 1740 in Fore Street. The eighteenth century grammar school in Queen Street has become a total ruin.

Lostwithiel has for centuries been pre-occupied with agriculture, but little else other than tanning. It is still an agricultural centre with the modern addition of a large milk-processing factory which draws its daily supplies from a large area.

What is to be the town's future in a fast changing world? It seems destined to get involved in Cornwall's vast tourist business. A pointer in this direction is a new motel, supplementing two or three long-established small hotels. Tourists, including those from the Continent, are beginning to look for accommodation at places inland, away from the congested coastal resorts. These have difficulty in catering properly and efficiently for the crowds that cram their streets in the holiday season. The frustrations experienced in trying to find a car parking space even at an exorbitant fee, or to enjoy a drink or a meal in reasonable comfort and in civilised surroudings, or attempting to buy something in a crowded shop, are turning people away from the seaside places.

Lostwithiel is too small and unsuitable to become a day-trippers' objective or a tourists' town, and it cannot offer the "attractions" that many people seek. But its quiet rural atmosphere will appeal to those whose interest is to sojourn at a central place from which to explore much of the county's still unspoilt landscape and coasts. It may not suit Lostwithiel to become such a centre although it is geographically well placed for that role. The steadily growing pressures from the phenomenal summer influx into Cornwall, bringing chaos and shabbiness with it, may become too compelling to resist.

The town is still unspoilt, an example of perfect conservation, the complete preservation of its traditional self. It gives the impression of not noticing the changes taking place elsewhere in Cornwall. It retains the perfect old-fashioned type of village shop and general store, where every customer is known to the proprietors and gets genuine personal attention. To cater in a competent and professional way for discerning holiday-makers Lostwithiel needs a face-lift, but not multiple or chain stores. These it could not support anyway. It also needs an improved and more extensive riverside promenade and park. To resort to the growing practice in Cornwall of setting up caravan and camping sites close to inhabited places would be unfortunate.

It is essential that Cornwall's most historic and best preserved small town shall not lose its character and its unique air of vintage maturity. Modern tourism should not be allowed to impose itself in the way it is imposing itself on places all round the Cornish coasts.

THE ANCIENT DUCHY OF CORNWALL

The Duchy of Cornwall was created by royal charter on March 17 1337. It replaced the Earldom of Cornwall and inherited all its possessions, revenues and palatine privileges. It comprised a large number of castles, baronies, lands and fees of many kinds both inside and outside the county.

In Cornwall there were Tintagel, Launceston, Trematon and Restormel Castles; the boroughs of Launceston, Lostwithiel, Tintagel, Helston, Camelford, Grampound, Saltash and Liskeard; more than two dozen manors with their many appurtenances, and the stannaries.

Outside Cornwall there were castles, baronies, lands and fees in many counties - Buckinghamshire, Devon, Hertford, Kent, Middlesex, Northampton, Oxfordshire, Surrey, Wiltshire and Yorkshire, with lesser holdings in other counties.

All these properties both in Cornwall and elsewhere were, by the charter, annexed and united in the newly created duchy, and it was enacted that they could never be alienated from it. Eventually some of the possessions were disposed of, and others acquired, but we are not concerned here with these changes, nor with the properties held outside Cornwall, except Sutton Pool harbour at Plymouth.

Prince Edward, the first son of Edward III, born on June 15 1330, became the first Duke of Cornwall, and was one of the very few princes ever to have had the honour conferred upon him after the moment of birth. Most subsequent dukes of Cornwall have assumed the title at the time of birth. The charter implied that only the first-born son of the reigning monarch can hold it. Should he not outlive the monarch the title cannot pass to the next or any other son, but lapses until the birth of the first-born son of the next monarch. During the interval the duchy with all its revenues reverts to the Crown. However, the charter has occasionally been interpreted differently.

The apparent reasons for the creation of the duchy were set out in the charter: briefly, to enable the duke to sustain the honour and dignity of his rank, and support the burdens and obligations devolving upon him by virtue of his position as the monarch's eldest son and as heir apparent to the throne. It was a question, as with all medieval kings and princes, of revenue. The Crown always saw its position and standing in terms of cash income.

The types of revenue from the Cornish holdings outlined above included the profits of the county and hundred courts; the prisage of wine at the seaports; the coinage or tax on tin; the farm of port dues and of tolls of markets and fairs; advowsons of churches and priories; income from parks, woods, chases; the letting of mills, ferries, river fisheries; rents from the tenements, farms and messuages (cottages and small holdings) of thousands of tenants, and many other minor sources of revenue. Probably the largest single item was the coinage or assay duty on all the tin produced and smelted in the county.

The real underlying reason for raising the earldom to a duchy was to help finance the new war against France that the king was planning. Edward III, in defiance of the Salic Law governing succession to the French throne, was claiming it through his mother, daughter of a French king. For him the only way to achieve this objective was to invade and conquer the country. Already he was ruler of the extensive duchy of Aquitaine which he held as vassal of the French king. The elevation of Cornwall to a dukedom was only one of a series of measures designed to strengthen England's war potential, but it was an important one.

Prince Edward was granted the Earldom of Chester soon after he was born in order that his newly created household be provided with the necessary income to maintain him and itself. The county of Chester was a true palatinate, and its entire revenues went to the infant prince's household. By the time the boy was seven his father was about to invade France. Cornwall with its mineral wealth, its maritime resources and Sutton Pool - the port of Plymouth which the duchy owned, and which was well situated for communication with Aquitaine - was much more valuable to the Crown than the earldom of Chester.

It was no coincidence that during the first ten years of the hostilities that began in 1337 the output of tin reached a higher level than was ever previously attained. The requisitioning of ships on a small scale and the recruitment of mariners in Cornwall for reasons of security and war purposes, especially against Scotland, had taken place on at least a score of occasions since 1300. But under the earldom the county's economic and maritime resources had never been fully exploited or utilised. Things were about to change.

Under the ancient earldom Cornwall had been to a considerable extent independent, enjoying privileges in the shape of a measure of autonomy and freedom from direct interference by the central government in many of its affairs. This sense of autonomy and separateness was now strengthened. From 1337, when Prince Edward was seven years old, until he died in 1376 the only forms of government known to Cornwall were, at first, that of his household and, later, of his council. The prince, known to history as the Black Prince, was destined never to become king, his father surviving him by one year. To be heir apparent to the throne every day of his 43 years of life was, to say the least, a unique circumstance in English history. He was to play the leading role in the new period of hostilities which became known as the Hundred Years' War. Cornwall was caught up in the crisis and was being geared for defence. It is known that the atmosphere was as tense as it was after Dunkirk in 1940, for the French king was preparing a counter invasion of England with forces stronger than Edward III's.

We can now take a look at the structure of the duchy in the fourteenth century when it fulfilled the purposed for which it was created. The household of Prince Edward's infancy and childhood grew larger as its responsibilities increased and became more complex with the creation of the duchy of Cornwall. It had to manage, in addition to the earldom of Chester, all the numerous castles, lands, estates, royal boroughs and other possessions in Cornwall and many other counties. In 1343 when the youthful heir to the throne became Prince of Wales and acquired territories in that country, it required more than a household organisation to run them efficiently in addition to the duchy of Cornwall and the earldom of Chester. Therefore in that year the council of Prince Edward was set up, taking over the responsibility of governing his manifold possessions. In 1362 he was created Prince of Aquitaine, the only prince ever to hold that title, which died with him. He took the greater part of his council with him to Bordeaux, leaving the rest to function at home with the help of the central government.

In 1343 the council quickly became a centralised system of government on similar lines to the King's Council. It welded the widely spread lands into a closely-knit whole. It was staffed by civil servants of high rank who were often trained in and drafted from the King's Exchequer and Chancery, the highest departments of state. The functions of the prince's council were advisory and to a lesser extent legislative and executive. Its ordinances had the effect of law within its territories. The council was flexible, and adapted itself to rule in the name of the prince the three distinct, separate and virtually independent territories: the earldom of Chester, the duchy of Cornwall and the principality of Wales, and eventually the fourth - the principality of Aquitaine. Each was governed as a separate entity according to its ancient traditions and customs, each under the supervision and control of experienced civil servants. Prince Edward thus became the direct ruler of large parts of England, Wales and France. His territories constituted individual states within the state.

In Cornwall the machinery of government worked more efficiently than in the average shire. There was a constant coming and going to and from London (and other places where the council happened to be) of officials, special commissioners, auditors and messengers. The king's ministers were excluded from the affairs of the duchy, but if in theory justice in the courts was still administered by the central government, it is significant that the itinerant justices who came to Cornwall for the assizes were also permanent members of the prince's council. There are on record at least three instances in which the prince over-ruled the king by instructing his officials to ignore or disobey orders issued to them by the King's Chancery, the highest court in the land.

The local administrative centre of the duchy was, as in the time of the old earldom, at Lostwithiel, where the county court, the headquarters of the stannaries, the maritime administration and the duchy Exchequer were situated. All the Cornish revenues were paid into this Exchequer. After local needs were met the balance was periodically taken to London, there to be collected by messengers from the prince's household at whichever of his manors in the home counties it happened to be sojourning. In 1343, with the addition of Wales to the household sources of revenue a permanent central Exchequer for all the prince's lands was established at Westminster, with his Receiver-General in charge of it.

Like each of the prince's territories the duchy had its own local staff to run its day-to-day business. The principal officers were the sheriff, the keeper of the prince's fees in Cornwall, the receiver, the steward, the warden of the stannaries, the havener, and a host of lesser officials - constables of castles, keepers of parks, the surveyor of game, the butler, bailiffs of the Hundreds, the stannary bailiffs, reeves of the manors and so on.

The most important duchy official during the lifetime of the Black Prince seems to have been the receiver, who had the responsibility of providing the wherewithal to help sustain the succession of military campaigns in France. For a period of three years - 1346 to 1348 - a Hanseatic merchant by the name of Tydman de Lymbergh held the office of receiver. At one stage in 1346 he was directed to send urgently several cargoes of tin to Flanders in vessels that were to be manned by archers for protection against hostile French ships. There can be no doubt that the profits from the sale of pre-empted tin contributed to the cost of the campaign that resulted in the victory of Crécy in 1346, which was followed by the siege and finally by the capture of Calais.

Cornwall's proportion of the total revenues from the prince's territories in England and Wales was probably at least one third. Professor T.F. Tout gives details of the average annual contributions from the various sources for the last three years of the prince's life. Cornwall's share was between one third and one quarter, and this was at a period when the largest part of the Cornish revenues - the coinage on tin - was in serious decline. Before this decline set in Cornwall's contribution to the prince's budget was probably greater than those of either Chester or Wales.[28]

Cornwall's virtual independence of the central government in the thirteenth and fourteenth centuries was not true self-government or real autonomy. It was a form of autonomy imposed from above as part of the king's design to strengthen the nation's war potential. If the creation of the duchy benefited the county's inhabitants in so far as it involved a revival of the economy, its tin-mining and ship-building activities, and provided more employment, it was intended for the ultimate benefit of the nation as a whole, not specifically for Cornwall's benefit.

This measure of autonomy has never been as great as it was during the first duke's lifetime. It has disappeared, but a desire for a limited measure of autonomy has persisted ever since, backed by a strong tradition of an ancient Celtic cultural background. This cultural background has tended to isolate Cornwall from the rest of England. Yet there has been no isolation from the outside world. All through the Middle Ages, and subsequently, seafaring and seaborne trade, as well as continental wars, have kept Cornwall in close touch with western Europe. The duchy's only hope of regaining even a limited or shadowy measure of autonomy would be through a strong national trend towards regional nationalism.

The Black Prince seems to have had little regard for the territories that provided him with the means to conduct his military adventures. He never visited his Principality of Wales, and only once did he honour the Earldom of Chester with his presence. He came to Cornwall three times, on each occasion sojourning at Restormel Castle. He did not go further west.

It is curious that in all the many formal letters and writs emanating from the prince himself, his ministers or from his council as a collective body, and addressed to duchy officials in Cornwall, during the forty years of his overlordship as duke, he is never named as the Duke of Cornwall, but invariably as 'the Prince'. All these letters, writs and ordinances have been published in the White Book of Cornwall.

THE BLACK DEATH PESTILENCE IN CORNWALL

The bubonic plague of 1348/9, better known as the Black Death pestilence, was the worst natural disaster ever to befall this country in historical times. It has been estimated that a third to a half of the population was wiped out.

Since medical science was as non-existent as hygienic habits there was no means of checking the spread of the terrifying epidemic. It was left to run its course. Reaching England from the Continent through the port of Melcombe in Dorset in August 1348 it crept over the whole land, penetrating the remotest districts. By the autumn of the same year it was devastating Devon, and in the following January it began to strike down the population of Cornwall.

Authentic factual evidence contradicts suggestions made from time to time that crowded towns suffered more severely than rural districts, or that Cornwall, a remote corner of the country, escaped the worst of the pestilence. Remote or not, it was probably more grievously afflicted than many other parts of England.

Let us take a typical district, the seaboard manor of Tewington belonging to the Duchy of Cornwall. It occupied a strip of the coast bordering St Austell Bay, about six miles long and up to a mile and a half deep, running north from Pentewan and then east to a point where Par Harbour now stands. It had a population that can be estimated at 350 to 400, made up of about 75 peasant families holding small farmsteads, and an unknown number of tinners.

With the rearing of sheep and pigs, corn growing, fishing and tin mining the manor had, by feudal standards, a well balanced subsistence economy. Subsistence, but no more. Being duchy property it was undoubtedly better organised and managed than most feudal estates, and had the advantage of an efficient system of accounting.

John Simond, reeve of the manor in the year of the pestilence, in preparing his accounts for submission to the duchy steward for the year ending at Michaelmas 1349, explained in writing why he had been unable to collect from tenants many of the rents and fines (acknowledgement money due to the landlord by conventionary tenants and fixed by convention at the assession courts held every seven years): "......for divers lands and tenements.... nothing here, because the said fines cannot be levied, by reason that the greatest part of the tenants are dead, through the pestilence happening this year before the feast of Easter; and the rest of the tenants who are yet living wish to leave their tenures by reason of poverty, if they cannot get a release of the same fines."[29]

From the nine *chevagers* (bondsmen of the lowest grade) who paid a penny a year acknowledgement money, Simond accounted for "2d for the *chevage* of two natives, and no more, because seven *chevagers* who were

55

accustomed to render yearly 7d, died in the months of April and May by the pestilence."

The rights of the Pentewan river fishery, the ferry that plied across the estuary (now silted up) from Par to Tywardreath, the common pasture land, dead wood, wild honey, turbary and the two corn mills, which were farmed out to tenants, all fell vacant "because the said tenants died by the pestilence."

In accordance with feudal custom the goods and chattels of the dead lessee of one of the corn mills, whose whole family had also succumbed to the plague, were seized in lieu of unpaid rent, but as no buyers could be found amongst the surviving tenants on account of poverty the dead man's personal belongings realised nothing.

We thus have evidence of an appalling situation with more than half the peasants dead. In simple and concise words the reeve, John Simond, a St Austell man of villein stock, thus unwittingly recorded for posterity the effects of the visitation of the plague that profoundly influenced the economic and social life of Cornwall right down to the Reformation. Two subsequent plagues occurring in 1361 and 1382 did not improve the situation. It would be possible to reconstruct on paper the manor of Tewington as it was in 1348. The names of the manorial tenants have been preserved, and many of the places where they had their messuages or tenements can be traced on a map of the present parishes of St Austell, Charlestown and Par.

The Tewington accounts for the years following the pestilence show that the Duchy steward endeavoured to re-populate the manor by offering to remit the fines or acknowledgement money to attract tenants, but also disclose the dire poverty in which the different categories of peasants existed. Even though a long period of relative prosperity had preceded the plague the tenants were still so impoverished that they could not scrape together the few pence or shillings with which to pay the farm or rent for the rights of the fishery, the ferry, the corn mills, pasture land and so on. The Duchy steward was compelled to re-let these rights at greatly reduced rents to prevent their falling into disuse or decay. And this at a time when the cost of everything, including labour, showed a sharp upward trend.

The hapless survivors of the pestilence, outnumbered by the dead and dying, could only turn to the Church for succour and comfort. This imposed a heavy burden on the clergy. If parish vicars were better able than the peasantry to resist the disease owing to their somewhat better nutrition and living conditions, they had to console the living, tend the dying and bury the victims. They knew the smell of death. Daily risking infection they played a true christian role in bringing what comfort they could to a helpless panic-stricken population. There is evidence that in Cornwall they suffered as severely as any other section of the community.

Cornwall was then part of the diocese of Exeter. The annual

56

number of new institutions by the bishop to benefices in the county tell an
eloquent story. Take a dozen years at random, including the year of the
pestilence, 1349:[30]

Year	Number of institutions	Year	Number of institutions
1330	11	1347	11
1335	13	1348	18
1336	15	1349	104
1337	15	1350	15
1343	12	1351	7
1344	12	1352	13

In 1348 with the plague ravaging half the country the number of
newly instituted incumbents in Cornwall reached eighteen, well above the
yearly average of thirteen.

The monthly institutions in 1349 reveal that the highest number of
deaths took place in the first six months, assuming that a few weeks would
have elapsed before the bishop found suitable incumbents to take over the
vacant parishes:

			C/f 58
January	3	July	15
February	3	August	7
March	8	September	11
April	14	October	6
May	13	November	6
June	17	December	1
	58		104

Thus by December, probably much earlier, the plague was over.
The numbers of new incumbents installed in 1350, 1351 and 1352 were
back to normal. If we deduct the annual average of thirteen from the total
of institutions made in 1348 and 1349 we find that about 96 incumbents
died through the plague. Thus, of the 175 parish and collegiate churches in
Cornwall, well over 50% lost their incumbents, thirteen of them twice.

At Bodmin priory the prior himself and eighteen of his twenty
canons succumbed. The two survivors were Roger de Honytone and
William de Tregawythan.

Throughout the duration of the pestilence John Grandisson, one of
the most able of Exeter's great medieval statesmen-prelates, remained at
his Chudleigh manor directing the affairs of his extensive diocese and
combating the demoralising effects of the terrible disaster. In Devon his
task was much more formidable than in Cornwall. In the first six months of
1349 he installed an average of thirty-four new incumbents each month,
compared with the normal average of less than three.

As parish after parish in the two counties became vacant newly appointed clerks - often several in a single day - came to him at Chudleigh for Admission. Grandisson had the greatest difficulty in finding sufficient qualified candidates, and he was obliged to appeal to Pope Clement at Avignon for dispensation to fill about 150 vacancies with acolytes and deacons.

The pestilence spread to the south-west and far west of Cornwall where we have evidence of devastation amongst the fishing communities, especially in the remoter parts of the Penwith peninsula. Smaller places such as Coverack, Porthallow and Sennen seem to have suffered more than the busier Mousehole and St Ives, and a few of them had to abandon their fishing activities for several years.[31]

The Duchy of Cornwall administration lost many of its officers who worked and lived in the county. It was found that the sheriff, two former sheriffs who had been receivers of the Duchy, and stannary and judiciary officials, and bailiffs had died without having paid large sums of money arising from their offices and functions. Some of these officials had farmed out their duties to other persons who had also died before having paid what they owed. For several years new duchy officers and travelling auditors from London were engaged in a widespread debt-collecting programme, tracking down the heirs of everyone who had died owing monies that would normally have reached the receiver through the established channels. Such was the feudal system: no matter how great the disaster or how many people had perished, the monies due up to the time of the plague had to be paid.

We have many illuminating glimpses of the effects of the plague. The duchy castles of Trematon, Launceston, Tintagel and Restormel soon fell into a state of disrepair for want of attention, whilst the open spaces in Restormel Park got overgrown with moss. The important tin mining industry, a valuable source of revenue for the Crown, remained stagnant for several years, but measures were taken to get it active again. In 1359 the Council of Prince Edward, Duke of Cornwall, addressed a notification to all his "lieges and subjects" in the duchy to the effect that certain tin grounds were henceforth reserved for the benefit of the prince, and that fifteen named tinners had been engaged to produce tin for a period of twelve months, and further that all other tinners and subjects of the Prince were to keep away from the said tin grounds.[32]

The mayor and burgesses of Lostwithiel, who leased from the Prince's Council the three borough corn mills, the fishery in the River Fowey and the port's maritime court, obtained a remission of half the annual rents of these rights owing to lack of business. In Cornwall as - elsewhere there were runaway bondsmen who fled to other manors in defiance of the Statute of Labourers, to obtain better terms of employment. One Ralph Vivian, a landowner in west Cornwall, in 1352 got

58

an affirmative reply to his appeal to the Prince's Council to order the return to his lands of several of his bondsmen who had illegally fled to the Isles of Scilly.

As the pestilence struck Cornwall in the spring it crippled the sowing season. It is certain that most of the corn and vegetable crops, such as they were, had to be left to rot in the ground for want of labour. There was consequently a shortage of food. In 1350 a ship at Fowey which had been loaded with a cargo of grain and other provisions for the English garrison at Bordeaux was boarded by a band of thieves. They took their prize to sea and, when off the Lizard, transferred the cargo to another vessel.

This robbery can be attributed to the widespread hunger that followed the pestilence. Much of the cargo was the property of Tydman de Limbergh, a merchant of Dortmund, who had been receiver of the duchy from 1347 to 1349 and who traded on behalf of Prince Edward. He was unpopular with tinners and merchants alike, since these had suffered from the exactions of his factors. In the Middle Ages it was not unusual to obtain redress of an injustice by taking the law into one's own hands.

THE PILCHARD

If any living creature is regarded in Cornwall as being one hundred per cent Cornish it is the pilchard. You only have to hear the word mentioned, and you visualise a Cornish fishing village. It has its place in the county's maritime history.

This little fish, a relative of the larger and more robust herring, and rarely measuring more than nine inches long when fully grown, is furnished with an unusually large supply of oil and bones. In an age less affluent than ours it was regarded by many as the poor man's fish. That was when nearly everyone in Cornwall - perhaps eighty to ninety in every hundred - was poor. It was therefore everyone's fish, certainly the most common and popular article of diet. It provided the people of Cornwall with a valuable health-giving nutriment. More than one traveller in the eighteenth and nineteenth centuries, after visiting Cornwall and then (as they still do) writing the inevitable book about it, commented on the healthy complexion and happy mien (as they no longer do) of young Cornish women, a condition arising from a diet consisting largely of pilchards.

As an article of commercial consequence the pilchard has now gone. It has deserted our shores, at least in the vast shoals of past centuries. It is still caught in small quantities, but no longer in hundreds of thousands, in millions, as formerly. Its place has been taken by the mackerel, although this fish is no stranger to the Cornish coast.

Cornwall benefited enormously from the pilchard. Its fishermen, and the coopers and packers who worked with them, earned their living for hundreds of years from catching, curing and exporting it. Uncounted millions, prior to Tudor times smoke-cured and possibly also salt-cured, and thereafter preserved only by salt-curing, were shipped to Italy, Spain and Portugal. And long before the age of cheap candles, of gas and electricity the pilchard provided us with an oil for lighting lamps.

The English Channel, the coasts of North Cornwall and southern Ireland were the northern limits of its travels, an indication that it does not like cold water. It was normally to be found half way up the Channel to Dover and down the Atlantic coast of Europe and beyond, as far as Madeira. We need not be concerned here with pilchards that have their habitat in other parts of the world.

The coming of the railway network linking Cornwall in 1859 direct with the Midlands and London had a great impact on the whole fishing industry, and produced many side effects. The railways opened up a large new market for fresh fish, including crabs, caught off the Cornish coast. The larvae of crabs were an important article of the pilchard's diet. A single female of one species of crab can spawn up to two million eggs. If pilchards in their vast shoals numbering millions had not devoured crab eggs in larval form as part of their normal diet the sea would long since have been cluttered with crabs.[33] The crab population could be maintained at a constant level if only a dozen eggs from every two million survived and became fully grown. The pilchard thus helped in no small measure to maintain the balance of nature in the regions it frequented.

Fewer crabs meant less food for pilchards, and it is believed that the numbers of pilchards frequenting Cornish waters diminished somewhat. But there was normally such an abundance of pilchards in the sea that the effects of a reduced diet were hardly noticed; there were pilchards to spare, and those left unfished were consumed by their natural predators.

The big rise in the price of pilchards after 1858 cannot be wholly attributed to any shortage of the fish, but partly to the growing demand from the rising population in Cornwall itself, and to the new demand from an extended English market, thanks to the railways.

Back in the years when pilchards were normally abundant they occasionally failed to appear where they might reasonably have been expected during the seining season. It was not then widely understood that the migrations of pilchards were determined by their food supply. It was not realised that their absence from a traditional area of the Channel meant that there was no food for them there. Such absence was described as "inexplicable."

The more localised unusual movements of pilchards were of course known to be caused by their natural enemies. These were porpoises, conger, hake and even mackerel, as well as sea birds such as gulls and gannets. Thousands of porpoises inhabited the English Channel. It needed only a small school of them to feel the desire to satisfy their appetite to sow panic amongst the shoals. These might then be chased and pursued into regions they would not normally visit, and forced to neglect a traditional area.

The pilchards that used to fill the seines of Cornish fishermen spent the winter in the English Channel. They did not go into the North Sea (unless chased there) where the water was too cold. Even the English Channel could be too cold in a severe winter. In the spring the pilchard moved out of the Channel, feeding in inshore waters as it progressed. It would sometimes travel well above a hundred miles out into the Atlantic where it found much of the summer food it needed, consisting of crab and other crustacea larvae, and the copepod, a minute form of marine life that was a constituent of plankton, which floats in large masses on the surface or at shallow depths.

In the autumn the pilchard migrated back into the Channel. In fine settled weather its return might be delayed. When there were disturbances caused by equinox gales - as sometimes happened - the pilchard hurried back. Until early in the present century large pilchard shoals frequented the north coast of Cornwall from St Ives to Port Isaac regularly enough to keep a large number of fishermen occupied at these two ports and at Newquay. They disappeared from this coast before the large shoals abandoned the south coast.

Pilchards had a habit of hugging the coast in shallow waters close to sheltered coves whether they were migrating outwards into the Atlantic in spring or returning in the autumn. Outgoing shoals that lingered for food and found it plentiful had no need to proceed any further. They stayed behind and provided the seiners with some out-of-season fishing. In these waters close to the shore where they fed on a type of seaweed the sandy inlets were ideal for seining.

Guided by signals from the huer or look-out man on a cliff a big rowing boat would pay out the long seine net in a wide arc, the starting end of the warp held firm by another boat. The plan was to trap the shoal between the net and the shore, and bring the net around to complete the circle where the two ends met. There was no escape for the fish since the net, suspended in shallow waters and kept down with lead weights, would be touching the sandy sea bed. Instead of getting caught individually in the meshes as in other types of net fishing the pilchards were encircled in the mass. They were scooped out of the seine by a small tuck net, and from there loaded by a flasket into the waiting boats that were then rowed the short distance to the shore. Occasionally the net, filled with fish, was hauled up on to the beach with the help of the villagers. When it was necessary to catch pilchards further out in deep water drift nets were used, the fish getting entangled in the meshes.

A big catch landed by either method was the occasion for rejoicing. The whole community would turn out - wives, sons and daughters - to get down to the job of 'bulking' the pilchards, which took place in the 'palace', a large building, often rectangular in design, specially constructed for the purpose. As many as five or six days were sometimes needed to bring in and bulk a catch numbering well above a million fish.

Bulking consisted of stacking the fish in long rows up to a height of about four feet, and about three feet thick, almost like a section of a thick wall. Each layer of fish was followed by a liberal layer of salt. These long stacks or piles were left standing a few weeks during which time some natural oil from the pilchards, mingled with bits of broken fish, scales, dirt and sometimes sand, was drained down the inclined floor into receptacles and sold as manure. Then the fish were cleaned with water one by one and packed into hogsheads, each layer of pilchards again being covered with a layer of salt. The pilchards in the filled hogsheads were then subjected to pressure by heavy weights in order to extract more oil. The yield could be anything from three to about eight gallons, according to the time of the year and the size of the fish, from every hogshead of about 3,000 fish. This by-product was sold as lamp oil, and formerly also for use as an ingredient in a sharp fish pickle.

The pilchard over the centuries seems to have changed its habits but little. Back in the Middle Ages the compact shoals came close to the shore in shallow water and were caught in seine nets in exactly the same way. By this method quantities far larger than were needed for immediate local consumption were netted and salted down or smoked for future use, and for export.

There is little evidence of the exportation of pilchards to foreign countries before the Tudor period, yet when that period arrived the export trade was already firmly established. The fish had acquired the nick-name 'fairmaids', a corruption of the word 'fumados', a description that was apparently current prior to the Tudor period, when the method of curing by smoking was said to have changed to that of salting.

At the middle of the eighteenth century exports, always to the same countries - Italy mainly, Spain and Portugal - reached their peak.[34] In the ten years from 1747 to 1756 an average of nearly ninety million pilchards a year were exported. In the nineteenth century there was a big decline in exports. In the fifty-seven years from 1815 to 1871 an average of over forty-nine millions a year were shipped abroad. This decline was partially compensated by a higher consumption in Cornwall.

It has often been said that the sardine is a young pilchard, and just as often that it is a separate species. Small pilchards were not frequently seen in very large numbers in Cornish waters, yet they were plentiful -and still are - off the French Atlantic coast where there has long been an important commercial sardine fishing and canning industry, all the way down the coast from Douarnenez to Royan, at the mouth of the Gironde.

Grilled sardines - at some places called royans - three to five inches long are a favourite dish to be found in most restaurants down the French west coast. Whether or not the French sardine is a different species from the Cornish pilchard, it is likely that it prefers the warm water of the Bay of Biscay to the English Channel. If it does grow to a full-sized pilchard it probably migrates to colder but still supportable water where its food is to be found in ample supply. The large sardine or pilchard is not commercially fished off the French coast.

About a hundred years ago it was reported that French fishery interests protected and cultivated sardines by seeking out the shoals and feeding them with cod roes. The fish liked this diet well enough not to migrate elsewhere.

The pilchard first occurs in Cornish documents in the thirteenth century. In Cornish waters its place has been taken by the mackerel. The fishing grounds of south-west England are now being over-fished, and may before long become as empty of mackerel as of the pilchard.

CORNWALL'S MOST SUCCESSFUL INDUSTRY

From its inception in the 1770's china clay production has been one of Britain's most successful smaller industries. Today this processed raw material produced in Devon and Cornwall enjoys an international reputation, and is exported to all parts of the world for use in the manufacture of an extensive and still growing range of industrial and household products. There is not a single home in Britain nor indeed in any other industrialised country in which china clay does not occur as a constituent in a variety of manufactured products.

The annual output reached only 30,000 tons by 1850. That was very slow progress for a period of eighty years from the 1770's. Then suddenly in the next twenty years to 1870 it was doubled twice to about 110,000 tons. Improved technology played no part in this phenomenal increase, which was made possible only by many new groups of adventurers or firms coming into the industry and opening up new pits, or clayworks as they were called. The old established firms also started up new clayworks. They cleared away the overburden, dug an open pit in the ground, laid out a primitive washing, sedimentation and air-drying system on the adjacent land, from which the gorse and heather first had to be removed, and then constructed wooden launders to bring to the site, across perhaps a mile of rough uneven country, a continuous flow of water for refining the clay. It was all very slow and laborious work. Under the old air-drying system the clay, with about the consistence of thick sludge, was cut into square blocks and transferred from the large open-air pans after the preliminary extraction of some of the water content, and spread out on the area cleared of vegetation, to be dried by the sun and wind until the moisture content was reduced to about ten per cent.

It was in this twenty-year period of astonishing growth from 1850 to 1870 that china clay was launched on to the world market. The high quality and the immense size of the Cornish deposit were getting known, and orders were coming in from countries as far away as India and the United States. Someone somewhere, reputedly in Holland, had discovered that the cost of producing paper could be appreciably reduced by incorporating china clay in its manufacture. It was necessary to replace only a small percentage of the fibrous raw material with china clay to give a paper mill a pecuniary advantage over its competitors. Although the idea was supposed to have been kept secret it spread to paper mills in other countries. A few mills were reported to have obtained supplies of clay anonymously through third parties to prevent it getting known that they were using this product to "adulterate" their paper. It was not known at the time that this "adulterant" did in fact improve the general properties, appearance and printability of paper. Such was the obsession for secrecy that not a single application was submitted to the Patent Office for a patent for using china clay in paper, although protection was granted to potters for different uses in porcelain, bone china and other types of ceramics.

The fast growing urban population in Britain, in other European countries and in the USA, the introduction of compulsory education and a rising standard of living all contributed to an insatiable demand for paper. In its turn the paper industry called for more and more china clay. There was plenty of clay in the ground, and it could be extracted by bringing more water to the site, but the problem was how to dry the refined product more rapidly. Under the existing air-drying system nearly twelve months passed before it was fit for the market. This meant that the producers had to pay out a year's wages and other operating expenses before they sold the dried clay, and as it was normal to grant several months credit to customers, about eighteen months passed before there was any return on the sale of the clay.

For about twenty years many experimental attempts were made to use artificial heat generated in kilns or furnaces fuelled by coal or wood. One of these was the invention by a certain Henry Daniell of St Austell. He deposited his specification with the Commissioners of Patents, and in 1853 was granted provisional protection. However, he failed to proceed with his application within the time set by the Act, and it lapsed.

The idea was to heat an empty chamber built over a furnace and use a fan to drive the hot air from it across a series of oblong shallow pans containing clay that had been partly air-dried but was still very damp, and thus draw out some of the moisture. The smoke and gases from the furnace were to be ejected through a flue, installed under the pans, to a chimney stack at the far end of the shed. The significance of the position of the flue was missed by Daniell, for the heat from it would probably dry the clay in the pans above it faster than the hot air blown across their surface. Daniell's idea was not entirely new, and it was developed by others. It became the flat bed type of kiln floor which the whole industry eventually adopted and which continued in use right down to the second world war, after which there was another significant revolution in the method of drying the clay with the introduction of various types of oil-fired mechanical plants. The flat bed kiln was the first major piece of new technology applied in the industry, and it completely changed its course.

In a flat bed kiln of average floor size about 200 tons of wet clay could be dried in a week, or up to 10,000 tons in a year, compared with only a thousand tons a year by the old air-drying system.

It needed only a few clayworks - and few firms could afford the capital outlay required - to change to the new system to bring about a sharp increase in the industry's output. For twenty years after 1850 the industry had struggled, and failed, to meet the fast growing demand. Then suddenly in the early 1870's production soared and exceeded the demand despite the fact that it continued to rise. There was a big surplus for which there was no sale. As we shall presently see, there was a reason for firms to continue producing clay that could not be sold.

Then in 1875 and 1876 production slumped by a third, simply because there was no room to store any more surplus output. There was unemployment, and several producers reduced clayworkers' wages, a move that provoked a brief but bitter strike. There was a second brief strike in 1876 when the clayworkers tried to form a trade union. Several producers cut their losses by selling their stocks for what these would fetch, even by auction. These sales had some relation to the incidence of financial difficulties that hit speculating newcomers to the industry.

By 1877 the crisis was over and the demand for clay stronger than ever, the output in that year being double that of 1870, which itself had been the highest ever.

One aspect of the industry contributing to the crisis was the law of the jungle that prevailed throughout British industry. The many new groups of adventurers that started producing clay in the 1850's competed against one another in the scramble for setts, giving the landlords the opportunity to play them off one against the others, thereby extorting exorbitant royalties. On some better grade clays these amounted to more than twenty-five percent of the selling price at the works. Also inexperience and lack of knowledge of the growing markets on the Continent made it impossible for newcomers to the industry to go out and find customers or to take advantage of the demand being greater than the industry's output. It was each for himself. Many small producers had no financial resources to weather the slump which they themselves had helped to bring about. They were ripe for bankruptcy. But the old-established partnerships, astute and knowledgeable, and employing continental agents who knew their job, came through the crisis as strong as ever.

Leases for china clay setts almost invariably ran for twenty-one years. The four to five dozen new leases taken up in the 1850's were coming up for renewal in the 1870's just when the slump arrived. Some producers holding these leases - whether new firms or old ones expanding their business - adopted the policy of "forcing the royalties", as it was called. Since royalties were payable to the landlords on the tonnage produced and not on the quantity sold, these producers forced their outpout to the highest possible level in order to be able to pay record royalties. There was no immediate sale for all their clay but they judged that their policy would put them in a stronger position to negotiate the renewal of their leases on more favourable terms.

The industry was first put on its feet by some of the leading Staffordshire potters in the period from 1775 to 1825, by which year most of them had pulled out again. Production was taken over by local traders such as the Loverings, Stockers, Wheelers, Martins, Higmans and

Martyns. These were able to finance their clayworks with capital they had accumulated from their normal trading as general dealers and shop-keepers. Amongst them were a hatter, a draper, a saddler, a tin smelter, a corn merchant and a maltster. They had a long start over the newcomers who began entering the clay industry in the 1850's, and had learned not only just where the higher grade clays were to be found, but knew the most effective way of laying out the extensive air-drying and refining installations. And they also knew where to sell their product to the best advantage.

Neither the landlords nor the parish authorities did anything very much to advance the interests of the local industry. It had to look after itself. In royalties and rates these two bodies between them took thirty per cent of the industry's gross revenue from the sale of clay. While the clayworks were heavily rated under the Poor Law system the metalliferous mines in the same area in the 1850's went rate-free. This was at a time when the mines, in spite of a severe depression, were much more important and employed many more people than the clayworks. During a period of three consecutive years in the 1850's eleven times as many miners as clayworkers were granted poor relief. The clayworks contributed no less than twenty-three per cent of all the rates, yet the mines paid nothing. The clay producers resented having in this way to support unemployed and destitute tin and copper miners. It was clear from the evidence taken before a Select Committee of the House of Commons on the rating of mines that there was something like a long-standing feud between the clay industry and the parish authorities, whilst the relations between the clay firms and their landlords were also not exactly of the best.[35]

The crisis of the 1870's constituted a clean and complete break with the past. There was no place in the industry any more for the small groups of adventurers whose method of financing a claywork was to call periodical meetings of the partners at an inn or a pub, when each of them would be asked to put £5 or £6 in the kitty to buy timber or tools, and pay the men's wages for the few weeks until the next meeting or until the money from an occasional sale was received. By comparison with the pre-crisis period capital investment was on a huge scale. To produce 10,000 tons a year at a claywork hitherto organised to dry only 1,000 tons involved the construction of entirely new refining installations, a new water supply, vast stone-lined and masonried settling tanks, a long kiln floor laid with hundreds of fire-proof tiles, a linhay or store and other buildings and water wheels. The welfare of the industry depended on the group of long-established firms who had become by far the largest and most enterprising producers. They enhanced its standing with their growing and discriminating clientele around the world.

Apart from the prolonged slump of the 1930's and the two world war periods the industry has not ceased to expand. From 200,000 tons of refined clay in 1877 output increased steadily to close on three million in 1977. Extensive research within the industry leads to more and more applications for this remarkable raw material. Advanced technology at all stages of production helped to make this possible despite growing competition from many sources of supply around the world. Skilfull marketing is another modern and essential attribute of the industry.

The china clay museum, established in 1974-5 at Carthew, about $2\frac{1}{2}$ miles north of St Austell, reflects the spirit of enterprise and progress for which the industry has long been known. It is an excellent example of industrial archaeology displaying the advance in production methods since the industry began.

THE AUTOBIOGRAPHY OF A CORNISH TRAVELLER

James Silk Buckingham was born on August 25 1786 at Flushing, barely half a mile across the water from Falmouth. His father, a native of Barnstaple, came from a family who had been seafarers for many generations. His mother was Thomazine née Hambly, of Bodmin. He described both his parents as being "decidedly of the old school in politics, sentiments and manners." James was the youngest of their seven children - three sons and four daughters.[36]

Before he was seven young James was sent away to a village school in Devon, about ten miles inland from Plymouth. The reason for this move away from the Fal estuary was to dissuade him from developing too strong a liking for the sea. He was the youngest of sixty pupils at the school. He wrote that the headmaster, teachers and senior boys were "all tyrants, the food revolting and insufficient, the beds hard and the clothing coarse." Gangs of boys had a habit of organising "bloody fights" amongst themselves. James spent a year of misery at this establishment and then returned home to attend his father's funeral.

He did not go back to the school. He spent two or three hours a day sailing and boating, and thereby acquiring, contrary to his mother's wishes, a taste for the sea. From this early age he was interested in everything that went on around him. Nothing missed his attention. He witnessed an angry demonstration by more than three hundred miners who had marched to Flushing where a cargo of grain was being unloaded into a warehouse. The war with France had forced up the price of bread and created a shortage. Then he was much impressed by the funeral of a family friend, and disgusted to see all the mourners, including the widow and the officiating parson, resorting after the burial service to an inn for "an abundant dinner" with a "profuse" supply of brandy, gin and rum. Everyone got drunk at this funeral.

Intoxication was then regarded as "not unbecoming", but rather the mark of a gentleman. It was a shabby sort of hospitality to allow any guest to leave the table perfectly sober. Marriages, christenings and funerals were made special occasions for even the poorest to indulge. The extensive smuggling of spirits and wine enabled all classes of people not only to drink duty-free but also to buy their liquor unadulterated.

Young Buckingham's passion for the sea was fostered by the presence at Falmouth of a squadron of warships under the command of Sir Edward Pellew, who had been a friend of his father. He was often invited aboard the Indefatigable, whose first lieutenant was related to his family by marriage. His mother very reluctantly agreed to let him take up a seafaring career. She had failed to persuade him to be trained for the Church, and although he tried hard to interest himself in this calling he could raise no enthusiasm for it. After further attempts had been made in the next few years to get him to study for this vocation he found it difficult "to reconcile the power, rank and riches of the Church, and even its forms and ceremonies, with the humility, equality, poverty and self-denial, and the disciples and apostles of Christianity, as well as with the character, conduct and precepts of its Divine Founder himself."

Once the decision to go to sea was made no time was lost. He attended a school at Falmouth which, in its time, it was customary to describe as an academy, since it trained some of its students for a particular profession; in this case navigation, but not at a practical level. This useful schooling lasted about a year. It was then arranged that although he was a mere boy he should join the crew of The Lady Harriett, one of the many Post Office Packet ships based at Falmouth. This vessel was on the regular Lisbon run, and the sailing master was the husband of James's eldest sister.

Still only nine years old he had the build of a lad of 14 or 15; he could handle a jolly-boat on his own; he could swim a couple of miles, and he was able to ascend "hand over hand" from the ship's deck to the main-top by a single rope. On the first two round trips between Falmouth and Lisbon he spent all his off-duty time studying the text books which, with his nautical instruments, made up a good portion of his kit. And he had many new experiences. His ship carried no official cargo, ostensibly transporting only mail and a few passengers. But there was a great deal of unofficial cargo. The whole crew from the captain down, engaged in large scale and well organised smuggling, each member being allowed, according to rank, from £5,000 worth down to £500 worth of merchandise that was easily saleable in Lisbon. Wholesale dealers established at Falmouth provided all this merchandise on credit. On the ship's arrival in Lisbon the Portuguese Customs officers came on board to settle the amount of the bribe to be paid by the captain and crew members to secure their connivance at smuggling the goods ashore. Everybody was in it - the Customs, the local clergy, the coastguards, the oarsmen of the midnight galleys that came alongside for the goods. It was much the same type of procedure on the return to Falmouth. Boats from the Isles of Scilly and Mounts Bay came out to meet the Packet and transfer goods ashore, or goods were slipped through the Customs at Falmouth at night. The Customs had no authority to board the Packet ships, which officially carried no merchandise. Yet duty was payable if the Customs happened to intercept this illegal traffic.

Young Buckingham took it all in. Smuggling, vice, corruption, dishonesty in officials.... human nature at its greediest: it all gave him his first real experience of the seafarer's life. The third trip brought him yet another new experience. The Lady Harriett was captured by an enemy (French) corvette. Her 6 six-pounders and 30 men were no match for the corvette's 30 eighteen-pounders and 300 men. In time of war the Falmouth

Incised Latin cross, Redgate, St. Cleer   *The Woolf-Greenham Collection.*

71

Latin cross, St. Pinnock   *The Woolf-Greenham Collection.*

72

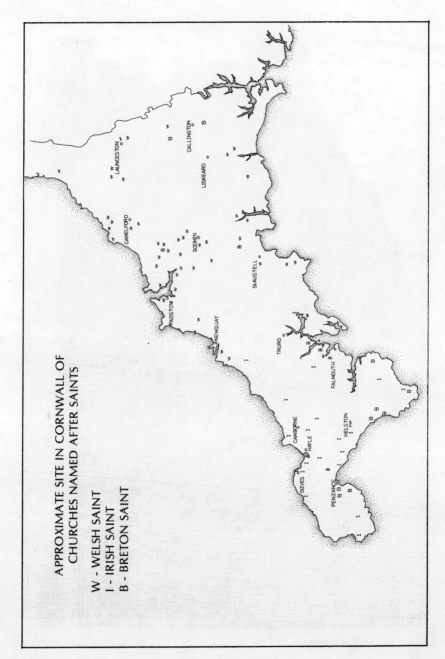

APPROXIMATE SITE IN CORNWALL OF
CHURCHES NAMED AFTER SAINTS

W - WELSH SAINT
I - IRISH SAINT
B - BRETON SAINT

73

Restored portion of stannary buildings erected in the thirteenth century.

Site of Lostwithiel's medieval quay.

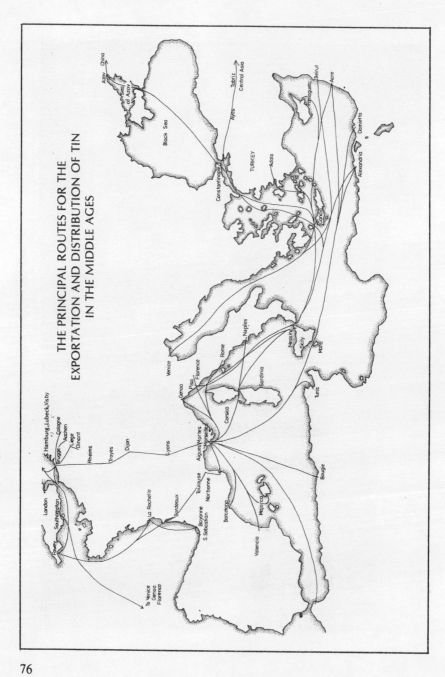

THE PRINCIPAL ROUTES FOR THE
EXPORTATION AND DISTRIBUTION OF TIN
IN THE MIDDLE AGES

Pilchard seine, Cadgwith, nineteenth century.

Restormel Castle, Lostwithiel.

Interior of Restormel Castle.

Lostwithiel's medieval bridge.

Lantern tower and spire of Lostwithiel church.

Newquay before the Tourist arrived. Fish curing cellars and coal trucks.

The Woolf-Greenham Collection.

Packet ships were armed, but their captains had orders not to resist capture if they were out-gunned.

The crew of the Lady Harriett were transferred to the corvette. It was found that this vessel had on board several renegade English mutineers and deserters from the warship Hermione in the West Indies. Her crew had mutinied and killed their officers who had "savagely" mal-treated them, and had then surrendered the ship to the Spanish authorities at Vera Cruz. The crew then dispersed and went their various ways, some remaining in the West Indies, others volunteering for service under the French.

With many prisoners from the Packet and other British ships, as well as her own compliment of 300 men crammed into the corvette the supply of fresh water had to be conserved. It could have been replenished by the vessel running to port, but the plundering of English merchant ships was too profitable an occupation to waste time in that way. There was a diabolical system of rationing the water to half a pint a day per prisoner for all purposes. Buckingham described it.

"A water-butt was placed before the mainmast, on its bilge, or lying athwart the deck. Into the bung-hole of this cask was inserted a long musket-barrel, with its muzzle at the bottom resting in the muddy deposit, which is sure to accumulate in all ships' water-casks that are stationary or at rest. The touch-hole of the musket-barrel was about three inches above or outside the bung-hole; and over this was a metal cap, secured by a padlock. The key of the padlock was placed in a small but secure iron box at the maintop mast-head, attached to the cross-trees. Every prisoner who wanted to drink had first to climb to the mast-head to get the key; then, after unlocking the cap over the gun-barrel, to suck as much moisture as he could, the first half-dozen mouthfuls being as much mud as water; and when he had slaked his thirst by the thin thread of water he could suck up through the touch-hole, he had to re-lock the cap, and take the key to the mast-head, there to be deposited for the next comer.... The result of this ingenious arrangement was that no prisoner ever went aloft for the key till he was so parched with thirst as to find it unendurable, while the muddiness of the deposit, and the extreme fatigue to the lungs and mouth in drawing up water through such a tube as a gun-barrel, soon tired the drinker and obliged him to desist."

Finally the corvette put into the Spanish port of Corunna where the merchant seamen were accommodated in a mansion. After several months the Spanish authorities, finding it too costly to feed people who were prisoners of the French and not their own, released them under armed escort. Buckingham, in a party of fifty, set out on foot on the 400-mile journey to Lisbon. Three hundred miles brought them to Abrantes, whence his party were taken the remaining 100 miles by barge down the Tagus to their destination.

Under escort as far as the Portuguese frontier the prisoners in their slow progess halted a few days at each of the principal towns -Santiago de Compostela, Vigo, Oporto, Coimbra - giving Buckingham the opportunity to acquaint himself with these very picturesque and historical old cities, the magnificent landscape of mountains, valleys and plains, the customs and condition of townspeople and peasants, their kindness and generosity, Spanish and Portuguese food and cooking, dress and so on. At night they were usually accommodated in stables belonging to inns.

In Lisbon the British naval press-gangs were busy rounding up all the British merchant seamen they could find to replace the casualties the fleet had suffered in a recent battle off Cape St Vincent in which several French and Spanish vessels were captured or sunk. Footsore men in Buckingham's party were seized, handcuffed and taken in boats out to the warships moored in the Tagus. Buckingham himself escaped into the open doorway of a house and up a flight of stairs where the occupants kept him concealed for three days until the press-gangs had gone. Then making himself known to the master of a Packet ship about to sail for Falmouth he was able to get back home.

There he found his mother determined that he should not go to sea again. The question of training for the Church came up once more, but this ten-year old youth knew that he lacked the necessary zeal, nor did he have "sufficient apathy or indifference to regard it as a mere mode of obtaining a livelihood." As he had a great passion for books it was arranged that he should be placed with a friend of the family who had a large bookselling and nautical instrument business at Plymouth Dock (now called Devonport).

He spent between three and four years at this job in which he was constantly in contact "with naval officers and seamen of every class; and their very recklessness had for me something irresistibly attractive." He had never seen such extravagance. After receiving their accumulated pay and their shares of money for captured prizes officers and men alike went on reckless spending sprees. The idea of laying some money aside for the future never entered their heads. Carriages of all types were in demand at enormous rates. Young midshipmen would spend as much as £200 in a week, and seamen would hire three or four coaches to remain on call on their stand. They were as "extravagant in clothes as in female favourites." The naval authorities did nothing to stop this reckless squandering of pay, for as long as a sailor had any money left there was no hope of getting him back to his ship or his duty.

At Plymouth much of Buckingham's time was spent visiting line-of-battle ships and frigates in the Sound, and vessels of all types undergoing refit in the dockyard. The theatres at Plymouth and Devonport which he often visited were always thronged with naval officers and sailors.

He was now at the age of fifteen and was suddenly filled with a sense of shame for having led a life of some gaiety and mis-spent his time. He felt a strong desire to repent. He knew he had disregarded his mother's wishes instead of repressing his inclination for a life at sea. He became deeply religious, and regarded himself as a rigid Calvinist. He had himself baptised by full immersion in icy water by a Baptist minister. He discussed at great length the irrationality of infant baptism, contending that it is not the function of a god-parent to speak for an infant in arms on the question of belief in the Christian doctrine.

One day young Buckingham was invited to take the place of a baptist minister who had been taken ill, and conduct a service for him. Unhesitatingly he responded, and without any preparation he preached an extempore sermon. Thereafter he was from time to time called upon by other ministers to stand in for them in case of illness or absence, either in Plymouth or its neighbourhood. Yet he felt it was sinful to prepare in advance any sermon he had to deliver. He must depend on what he believed to be inspiration that would come to him at the time it was required.

In due course the pendulum began to swing back the other way, and the call of the sea again became strong, with a parallel weakening of his religious zeal. In twelve months he was back to a normal state of mind, and volunteered for naval service. He was accepted. Although he was strong and active, and willing to discharge all his duties, he discovered in himself a revulsion against the tyranny and cruelty exercised on many members of the crew of his ship. Since most of the crew had been press-ganged, some of them dragged from their beds at night, others removed from merchant ships where they got more than double the naval pay, there was sullen discontent and "silent brooding of revenge." From dawn until the evening gun, which was the signal to return to their hammocks, the men were full of "dogged obstinacy."

Two incidents that Buckingham was compelled to witness caused him to decide to desert. One was the hanging of a mutineer at the yard-arm of a frigate anchored in Barn Pool, a punishment which had by order to be witnessed by one boat's crew from every naval ship in port. The second was the flogging a deserter round the fleet. This victim, a civilian, had been dragged by a press-gang from his home, wife and children in the dead of night. According to Buckingham he then did the most laudable thing in the world: he escaped back to them again. On his recapture he struck the officer who seized him. For this misdemeanour he was told he could have been hanged, but instead he was awarded the lighter punishment of flogging. His outstretched arms and legs were lashed to a wooden framework in the launch in which he was taken from ship to ship, at each one to receive twelve lashes of the cat-o-nine-tails on his bare back. His own crew mates had to man the launch, in which was also his own ship's surgeon, whose responsibility was to ensure that the punishment was stopped before death was inflicted. The man's back was soon a mass of lacerated flesh and blood. The punishment was repeated alongside about ten ships before the surgeon called a halt. The man died on the way to hospital.

Young Buckingham deserted while in charge of the ship's jolly-boat at Mutton Cove, with only sixpence in his pocket. It took him three days to reach his home at Flushing after luckily avoiding recapture by a press-gang at Liskeard. All the members of his family did their utmost to prevent him from going back to sea. It was decided that he should train for a career in the legal profession, and he was articled to a Mr. Tippett, Falmouth's leading attorney. Once more, after a period of a year, he decided that he could not continue in that profession. His "straight-forward and unsophisticated mind" could not comprehend "the positive mis-statements and deception practised on clients and witnesses", nor could he approve of "so much feasting and carousing at the principal hotels at the expense of suitors."

For the next two years he was without employment, and studied music under a negro musician who was an excellent composer and violinist, and who taught several other instruments. Young Buckingham persevered, having daily one hour's tuition and four hours' practice, and within six months acquired enough competence to be invited to play first flute at a concert given in Pendennis Castle by a military band. His other activities in this period of ease and pleasure included reading, riding, boating and writing poetry. A family friend, the commander of a Revenue cutter, invited him to join the vessel on a smuggler-hunting cruise. During his absence at Milford Haven on this trip he learned of his mother's death.

The whole of her property was bequeathed in trust equally to James and his two unmarried sisters until he came of age. He was still only eighteen. The property, comprising houses, lands, shares in mines and fisheries, and several small coasting vessels, would meanwhile yield for the three beneficiaries sufficient income to live in comfort and without anxiety for the future. During the year of mourning for his mother he fell in love with Elizabeth Jennings, daughter of a once wealthy farmer who had become bankrupt through unwise investment in land and livestock. Jennings's sons had taken up the seafaring profession.

James and Elizabeth were married at St Gluvias church in February 1806. Prior to this event he had obtained a promise of an advance of capital from the trustees of the estate to establish a business at Falmouth. Once married he felt he would have no desire to pass most of his time away at sea. A married man's place was at home. The business was to comprise the sale of nautical and astronomical instruments, marine charts for all parts of the world, a printing office and a library. The trustees approved the scheme, and recommended that the requisite supplies and equipment for starting up the business be ordered on the usual terms of six or twelve months credit, by which time they would be able to provide the funds to meet the

86

outlay. Buckingham went ahead and set up the business. Here he learned the craft of a typesetter and printer.

Before the period of credit had run out one of the trustees got control of the whole management of the estate into his own hands. He could not resist the temptation to make a big fortune for himself by purchasing the entire cargo of a Swedish vessel from the East Indies and smuggling it ashore. The vessel had called at Falmouth ostensibly for repairs and provisions, but in fact to sell the cargo clandestinely. The trustee, and four other accomplices with him, had to raise the cash and hand it over before the merchandise was transferred from the Swedish ship outside the harbour at night to waiting boats. He had obtained the money against the security of the family property with which he and the other trustees had been entrusted, in order to invest the proceeds in this smuggling speculation. The plan failed, the Revenue officers intercepting the smuggled goods as they were being landed at points along the shore. James Buckingham, his wife and his two unmarried sisters were left penniless.

Stunned by this calamity he had no choice but to go back to sea to make a living. He decided to go to London to meet his wife's second brother Thomas Jennings, master of a West Indiaman, in the hope of being offered a job on his ship. He obtained a free passage to Dover by working his way aboard a coasting vessel. From Dover he walked to London in three days and lodged in a garret at 2/6d a week. Learning that his brother-in-law's ship was delayed and was not expected for three months, James got a job as a compositor at a printing works, making use of the skill he had acquired in his own printing office at Falmouth. Although he earned no more than fourteen shillings a week he lived sparingly and managed to send his wife a Bank of England one pound note at the end of each month.

He soon got tired of London, disliking the noise, the dirt, the fogs, his fellow workmen and city life generally. He decided to go to Oxford on the recommendation of a colleague who told him about the Clarendon printing works there. He found lodgings in a garret at 1/6d a week. He had to accustom himself to a very stringent diet. His breakfast was normally a small loaf of bread with a basin of milk; for dinner he had potatoes and a little butter; tea was rice pudding. The only meat he ate was a mutton chop on Sundays. Now earning a pound a week he was able to send his wife a one pound bank note every fortnight.

Then came news that Captain Jennings's vessel was expected any day. Buckingham gave up his job at Oxford and went back to London. He wrote his wife, in answer to her request, to join him there, and bring their infant daughter with her. He had to sell some of his few belongings to pay her fare.

Captain Jennings's vessel was further delayed, and Buckingham had to get another job as compositor at a works where Horsburghs East

India Directory was printed. In due course, when the vessel arrived, the Buckinghams were able to move into more comfortable lodgings. Within a month or so James was appointed chief officer of the Titus, his brother-in-law's new vessel, ready to sail for Trinidad. The outward trip was uneventful but the vessel experienced two hurricanes, one when at anchor at Trinidad, the other off the Newfoundland Banks on the return journey home when the convoy in which the Titus was travelling got entangled with another convoy. When daylight came it was found that eight ships were missing, believed foundered with all hands, and that 33 of the remaining 45 had had their masts carried away.

After a brief spell back in London Buckingham met another Jennings brother - John - who had become a naturalised American. He had been trading across the Pacific to China, and had now purchased a vessel to trade in the Atlantic. He took on Buckingham as his chief officer and sailed to Norfolk, Virginia. Some very agreeable weeks were spent there amongst American seafaring people. Buckingham was much impressed by the lack of class distinction and by the spirit of equality existing between officers in the navy and those in the merchant service. By contrast British naval officers looked down with contempt on British merchant navy officers.

Back in London again Buckingham, having now qualified for a command, was appointed master of the Surrey, a West Indiaman, and sailed to Nassau in the Bahamas. Here he met with corruption and smuggling in the Spanish Main and Central America. All trade was illegal contraband trade. Normal legal trading was non-existent. Consequently Spain, and her colonies in this region, were so impoverished from the lack of Customs revenue that everybody was heavily taxed, a circumstance which in turn generated rebellion and led to the independence of the colonies.

It was now 1811 and Buckingham was twenty-five years old. During his next spell in London he paid frequent visits to Lloyds and the Royal Exchange, but had little use for the mercantile society he found there. Ships' captains, brokers, merchants and ship-owners conversed in a language he did not understand: the rise and fall in prices, fluctuations in sea freights, speculation, the tricks of the trade and so on. Their reading was confined to newspapers, shipping lists and prices. Although he found their hospitality in matters of food and wines generous and agreeable, they were "uncultured and knew nothing of new literary works, scientific discoveries, art, religion, music, operas or other products of culture."

Buckingham resigned his command of the Surrey because he refused to make a false declaration for the underwriters regarding damage caused to his ship when colliding with a sunken wreck on the Goodwin Sands. He was told that however good a seaman he might be he did not know his duty to the owners in whose service he worked. For so young a master to impair his future prospects by refusing his co-operation was proof that he was wholly unacquainted with business. He learned too that generally underwriters and ship-owners had a financial interest in the total loss of their ships. On this question he was extremely forthright and outspoken.

He now turned his attention to the Mediterranean and was offered a job as master of the William, owned by a French company. At this period it fell to the captains of ships to recruit their own crews, which he called "a disgusting task." Disgusting because it meant combing the dens of crimps in the alleys of Rotherhithe, Wapping and other places down the Thames. Seamen were hard to get even at high wages, since the press-gangs were busy rounding them up for naval service. The crimps made a business of fleecing seamen coming off ships newly arrived in the Thames, promising them prostitutes and good accommodation for the duration of their stay in port. On the strength of such promises many seamen parted readily with much of their accumulated pay with which they came ashore. The crimps sold them cheap liquor, got them drunk and robbed them. Many a drunken seaman was pushed into the murky night waters of the Thames to drown.

His experience of dockland crimps led Buckingham to press for the establishment of sailors' homes at all ports in Britain and the United States. His campaign was eventually successful when in due course he became a Member of Parliament, and was chairman of a Select Committee of the Commons on shipwrecks.

For reading matter on his first Mediterranean voyage he bought about a hundred books on all the countries bordering that sea and the Black Sea. During extended calls at both Gibraltar and Valetta he made it his business to meet many people and discuss all manner of questions with them, whilst taking in everything he heard and saw. From Malta he proceeded to Smyrna, his final destination. The agent to whom the ship's cargo had been consigned introduced him to the social life in which the Europeans indulged. It provided him with useful business and social contacts to follow up on his return to London.

When it was necessary Buckingham never failed to assert his rights, even when it might bring him into conflict with authority. As his ship was well armed with twelve guns, musketry and small arms he offered, before sailing from Smyrna to return home, to escort any small unarmed vessels about to proceed westwards, as a protection against the pirates that swarmed off the Greeek islands. When ready to raise anchor he gave the recognised official convoy signals, including the firing of a gun. For this he was taken to task by the captain of a British naval frigate that had just arrived in port, and summoned to the frigate to account for this irregular conduct.

"How dare you, sir, to make signal for convoy, not holding His Majesty's commission as a naval officer?"

To which Buckingham replied: "Sir, I not only dare to do so now, but to repeat it if required: and I dare you to haul down such signal at your peril."

Buckingham stood his ground, maintaining, successfully, that he knew of no law or authorised regulation by which an armed merchant vessel was forbidden to offer protection to unarmed ones which chose to sail under her convoy.

Back in London, furnished with introductions from Smyrna, Buckingham began a continuous round of social activity - dinners, musical evenings, balls, operas, theatres and parties until it all became wearisome. He longed to get back to sea. The William's owners sold their vessel, and Buckingham obtained command of a larger ship, the Scipio, which would take him back to Smyrna. His second daughter, aged six months, having died at the end of his three months' stay in London, he arranged for his wife and first daughter to accompany him. The Scipio sailed in a convoy of more than 200 ships.

No longer in convoy after leaving Malta the vessel was attacked by two pirate ships and a running fight took place. Armed with 10 twelve-pounder carronades the Scipio eventually won, but suffered considerable damage. One pirate ship was sent to the bottom and the other sheered off, severely battered. Buckingham made no attempt to pick up any pirate survivors swimming or struggling in the water. His philosophy was that their fate was the consequence of the kind of life they had chosen to follow.

As female visitors from England rarely came to Smyrna Mrs Buckingham attracted much attention, and aroused sufficient interest in the Turkish Governor's circle to be invited by the chief lady of his harem to spend a day there as her guest amongst the beautiful Georgian and Circassian girls. The Scipio's return voyage to England was uneventful.

Buckingham had now accumulated sufficient capital to retire from active seafaring and consider establishing a business in Malta as a merchant and ship-owner. The island had become the busiest trading market in the Mediterranean, following Napoleon's blockade in attempting to close all European ports to British shipping. Malta was a main base from which merchant vessels, protected by the navy, were breaking the blockade.

Having decided to settle with his family in Malta Buckingham used all his capital to buy a cargo of merchandise and shipped it in a vessel in which he travelled as passenger. His wife and daughter would join him once he had established his business and found a house for the family. When the convoy was within a day's sail of the island it was intercepted by a warship bringing the news that the plague had broken out there. Ships with government stores were then ordered to avoid Malta and proceed to Minorca; other vessels could go where they chose, including Malta.

Buckingham left his cargo with the ship's agent on the island and proceeded to Smyrna to wait there until the plague had abated. But it was

90

not to be. Every week the news from Malta got worse. The warehouses in which his merchandise had been stored had to be burnt down because all the people employed there had died of the plague. There was no possibility of recovering anything from the insurers, and Buckingham found himself left with £100, and a wife and daughter to keep.

He had heard that the Pasha or Governor of Egypt was planning to employ Europeans to work in his service. From friends at Smyrna he obtained letters of introduction to the British Consul-General in Egypt and then sailed to Alexandria, whence he proceeded to Rosetta to travel up the Nile to Cairo. He used his leisure time to improve the knowledge of Arabic he had picked up in Malta and Symrna. And all the time his mind, restless and penetrating as ever, took in the scenery, observing the smallest details of dress, food, customs, even the style of working of the Nile ship's crew. Nothing within eyeshot or earshot escaped him. In Cairo he was luxuriously accommodated in an apartment at the British Residency, and while awaiting an introduction to the Pasha he spent his time in sight-seeing and attending parties and dinners.

As the Pasha was absent on a military campaign in Arabia he had left his confidential agent, an Armenian, to discuss matters with Buckingham. The first problem to resolve was the transfer from Alexandria to the Red Sea of two American brigs the Pasha had bought. The agent was hesitating to send them around the Cape of Good Hope since he had been informed that the British East India Company would seize and confiscate all vessels found east of the Cape without their licence. Never wanting for ideas Buckingham offered to take the two ships up the Nile to Cairo, strip them down to their bare hulls and then haul them, mounted on specially built carriages, using teams of camels or horses, across the desert to Suez.

Another question was the possibility of re-opening the ancient trading connection between India, Egypt and the Near East. This would involve the construction of a canal between the Red Sea and the Mediterranean. According to classical writers, such as Herodotus, Strabo and Pliny, a canal had existed in the time of the kings of ancient Egypt, and it had already disappeared by Roman times. Awaiting the Pasha's decision on his proposals Buckingham set out on a round trip of about 350 miles up the Nile, then 100 miles east across the desert to the Red Sea port of Quseir, and then north to the Gulf of Suez where he would carry out a hydrographical survey.

In Upper Egypt he met with a caravan of slaves from Central Africa being shipped down the Nile to Cairo. He described the caravan: "Nothing could be more wretched than the condition of the poor captives; some quite infants, others decrepit from age, and a large number of the male youths castrated to serve as eunuchs in the harems of the Turks, whilst the females were rigidly guarded, and their chastity preserved by means which were most cruel, but cannot with propriety be described."

Then he came to the ancient city of Thebes where he remained several weeks, and where he met and became a good friend of the Swiss explorer Johann Ludwig Burckhardt. He had been warned that the 100-mile journey across the desert to the Red Sea would be perilous. It was. The warning was no exaggeration. At night he and his Albanian guide took turns at keeping watch for thieves. One night his guide got drunk while on duty, and allowed their camels, muskets and pistols to be stolen. The next morning Buckingham refused to turn back. He managed to persuade a Bedouin to part with two donkeys, and then continued his journey. Having come thus far he was not going to give up. "It was," he wrote in his diary, "a perseverance bordering on obstinacy, but I had often found that such a spirit was the only one by which great difficulties could be overcome."

The next day - Christmas Day 1813 - Buckingham and his sullen guide were stopped by a group of mutinous Albanian soldiers serving in the Turkish army and returning from Quseir. The guide told the soldiers that he himself was travelling alone and had nothing to do with the Englishman. He at once went on his way and was out of sight before the soldiers decided what to do with their protesting British captive. They eventually let him go free, but only after tearing his safe-conduct to shreds and robbing him of everything, including his clothes and footwear. He was left standing completely naked in the desert. "It was," in his own words, "no time for despondency."

A wandering Bedouin came along and gave him a garment of rough goat hair. Together they reached Quseir where Buckingham met the Italian agent to whom he had been recommended before setting out from Cairo. He learned that there was serious trouble in the town, and it would get worse as more demoralised and mutinous troops landed from boats bringing them from Arabia where the Pasha's campaign was not going well. Buckingham gave up the project of carrying out a hydrographical survey, and made his way back to Cairo.

His next task was to try and trace the bed of the canal first dug in pre-historic times across the desert. As always, the journey was a new adventure for him. Dressed as a Bedouin he set out with his party in a vast caravan crossing the desert from Cairo to Suez: 4,000 camels, 20,000 people, a great variety of races, costumes and colours. Exploring the desert north from Suez to the lakes and then westwards to the Nile, Buckingham discovered traces of the course of the ancient canal. His findings corresponded with the measurements giving by Herodotus, who died in 424 B.C.: the canal must have been about 100 feet wide and 30 feet deep, large enough to take two triremes abreast. Owing to intensive cultivation the junction of the canal with the Nile had long been obliterated, but it had been near Zagazig, about fifty miles north of Cairo.

The spring and summer of 1814 Buckingham spent at Alexandria, giving him an opportunity to explore the delta of the Nile and to improve his knowledge, including his Arabic. He never missed a chance to talk to people close at hand, no matter who they were. When on a trip on an open un-decked wheat boat on the Nile he noticed that at every village very large flocks of pigeons came and settled on the uncovered wheat, filling their stomachs and gizzards. The man in charge of the boat sat placidly doing nothing to prevent the loss of his wheat. When questioned by Buckingham he replied that pigeons, as well as men, were God's creatures and had to eat. This did not seem sensible to Buckingham who commented that it was uneconomical to lose so much wheat in that way, since it would not be difficult to place a cover over the cargo.

"If," said the boatman, "all the wheat boats reached Alexandria with their cargoes intact there would be a glut of wheat on the market and the price would go right down. But if they arrived with half their cargoes eaten by the pigeons there would be a shortage, and the market price would rise sharply. In fact I shall get as much money for half a cargo as for a full cargo. I shall be satisfied, and the pigeons are satisfied."

Then came the first personal meeting with the Pasha. The two men, in the presence only of the Armenian confidential agent, discussed commerce and navigation, mainly relating to India. Buckingham suggested that the superiority of England, America and other western nations over Africa and Asia was the result of education, which led to the extension of knowledge and discovery in all directions - in agriculture, mining, manufacturing, geology, chemistry and so on. Egypt should educate its young men aged from 16 to 21, sending them to western countries to learn English or French, and to be trained in commerce and in industries likely to have a future in Egypt. Buckingham also advised the Pasha to import high quality cotton seed from the southern American states to improve the quality of Egyptian cotton, and so build up the local industry.

The Pasha dropped the idea of cutting a canal to link the Red Sea with the Nile because he had been warned in Arabia that the British would use the canal as a stepping stone to turning Egypt into a colony, and this would not be to the advantage of Egyptians, but only enrich the British still more. Buckingham failed to shift him from this point of view.

Since Buckingham had decided to go to India on behalf of a British mercantile firm established in Egypt the Pasha gave him a commission to buy some ships to start up Egyptian trade with India. This would save the expense of transporting his two ships across the desert from Alexandria to Suez.

Buckingham travelled to Suez and joined thousands of Mecca pilgrims waiting for boats to take them down the Red Sea to Jedda. He obtained a berth on a dhow carrying more than two hundred men, women and children, and some horses. The conditions on board were primitive even for that period. Buckingham bought a coil of spare rope carried by the dhow, and from it made himself an improvised device not unlike a hammock which he slung over the stern, and which could be lowered or hoisted by a double-block tackle over which he had sole control. He thus spent his days in the shade of the stern away from the noise, filth, vermin, insects, heat and over-crowding. And he could lower himself into the water whenever it suited him to do so.

One night a sudden and violent tropical storm broke out, and the dhow, anchored as usual for the night, dragged her only anchor. Buckingham advised the captain to take the ship away from the coast he had been hugging all day and stand out to sea to ride out the storm, but he refused. There was panic among the screaming passengers, the horses stampeded and the crew rushed to and fro between stem and stern trying to carry out the captain's contradictory orders. In the end the dhow survived, but five men were drowned. Buckingham lost most of his luggage, cash and papers. Then he was taken ill with a fever. After another ten days the vessel reached Jedda.

Buckingham remained here two months as the guest of the English Agent, who was deputising for the British Consul. He sailed from Jedda for Mocha on 14th January 1815 and eventually arrived at Bombay on 6th April. His autobiography contains descriptions of life at the two busy Arabian ports, both of them thronged with many types of Africans and Asians living and trading there.

Although he had lost his introductions to several people at Bombay copies had been sent overland via Baghdad and Basra, and were awaiting him. He tried to persuade Bombay merchants - mainly British nationals - to trade with Egypt, but they all professed a complete lack of trust in the good faith of the Pasha. He was given a better reception by British civil servants, and found the door to élite Bombay society wide open to him. ".... the Civil Service constitutes a caste of aristocracy within whose barriers the military officers are only sparingly admitted, except those of highest rank, merchants only of the first class, and merchant-captains and traders never."

Buckingham attended "endless dinners, balls and concerts." It seemed to him that with all the complaints he heard in Bombay about exile from home, heat, mosquitoes and many other grievances ".... there was no place under the sun that I had ever yet visited where the art of enjoying the present was so fully understood and practised as it was here...."

In spite of all the gaiety and pleasure of this kind of life Buckingham did not lose sight of one purpose of his visit. But he began to despair of interesting the merchant community in opening up trade with Egypt and the Mediterranean. If there were a treaty embodying certain guarantees the situation might be different. However, his main concern was to ensure a living for himself and his family back in England. He obtained command of a 1,200 ton ship newly launched near Bombay, owned by the Imam of Muscat, to trade between India and China, and had been offered what he described as a handsome salary.

The appointment attracted attention, and aroused envy amongst ships' officers who had applied for it and had been turned down. One of them had heard that Buckingham did not hold the East India Company's licence to visit India. The fact was reported to the Governor of the Company, who sent for him. He was "polite, dignified and polished", a man who appealed to Buckingham. He remarked that Buckingham could pass for an American, especially as he had just told him that he had been to America. Buckingham commented that he was born and bred an Englishman and had no particular desire to be, or to be taken for, an American. "Well," said the Governor, "if you will not be an American I cannot of course make you one." They parted good friends, but Buckingham, who incredibly had missed the point, was a little puzzled.

His friends told him that if he were American (or for that matter any nationality but British) he would be able to obtain the Company's licence to remain in India and keep his job as captain of the new 1,200 ton ship. Only Britons were affected by the East India Company's monopoly. The Company feared that Britons trading independently would undersell them in their own markets.

On 10th May 1815, one month after his appointment as captain of the Imam's vessel, Buckingham received formal notice to quit India. He did not take this banishment order lying down. He spent the next seven weeks appealing again and again to senior officials up to the Governor himself to be allowed to remain. It was all in vain. He had to leave, although he had made many friends, including some who were involved in expelling him from the country. They were personally sorry to see him go.

He sailed from Bombay at the end of June 1815, reaching Suez only on 20th November. He spent much of these five months carrying out a hydrographical survey of areas of the Red Sea, taking soundings; recording tides, currents and winds; locating coral reefs; making plans of good anchorages; correcting errors in an existing chart and calling at every port between Mocha and Suez. His MS journal of this voyage occupied more than 500 folios, equivalent to 1,000 printed book pages.

Back at Alexandria he met the Pasha and explained to him that the only obstacle in the way of a revival of trade with India was the want of an official convention that would guarantee to merchants in Bombay full protection for their goods during transportation and storage against pirates at sea and thieves in the Egyptian desert and on the Nile. And there should be a big reduction in the existing Customs duties.

The Pasha agreed, and a Convention was drawn up. Buckingham

was to take it to Bombay for ratification and signing. Invested by the ruler of Egypt with diplomatic status as his Envoy, and with authority to purchase ships and handle cargoes on his behalf, Buckingham went back to India overland via Baghdad. The East India Company would not dare expel the Envoy of a friendly country.

The decision to return to India in 1816 as the Egyptian Envoy completes the first two volumes of Buckingham's autobiography. They cover his life only to the age of twenty-nine, and were both published in 1855. Then he died.

Few people in his time could have had such a full or a more adventurous and satisfying life than James Silk Buckingham. His autobiography, often flamboyantly Victorian in style, and sometimes naive, is a valuable social and historical document. It recounts significant incidents and personal experiences, and contains observations on many aspects of the human condition, human suffering and pleasures, the things that characterise countries and peoples but which historians and biographers do not personally experience. Buckingham is a true historian of the period in which he lived. He records nothing that is trivial.

His subsequent career from the age of twenty-nine onwards was just as varied and tempestuous. A brief summary must suffice here.[37]

From 1818 until 1822 he was editor of the Calcutta Journal, but the opinions which it expressed displeased the East India Company. In 1823 he was expelled from India, and returned to England. For various periods from 1824 to 1834 he was editor of the following literary or political reviews:

The Oriental Herald & Colonial Review
The Sphinx
The Athenaeum
The Parliamentary Review

From 1832 to 1837 he was Member of Parliament for Sheffield, and made his presence strongly felt through many speeches and sitting as chairman or member of several House of Commons Committees.

He gave up his seat in Parliament to become a professional lecturer, and accepted invitations to address the United States Senate and other bodies at Philadelphia, New Orleans and New York, the Quebec Parliament, the Athénée Royal and the Chamber of Deputies in Paris. He made vigorous speeches in many parts of Britain on a vast range of subjects from free trade, public health and temperance to civil liberties and education. His quarrel with the East India Company over their trading monopoly went on year after year and was not finally resolved in his lifetime.

Buckingham was a prolific writer, publishing more than two dozen volumes as well as numerous short works, reports, booklets and tracts in support of his manifold interests and activities. His works included the following travel books, most of them in two or three volumes:

Travels in Palestine
Travels amongst the Arab Tribes East of Syria & Palestine
America, historical, statistical, descriptive
Travels in the northern states of America
The Eastern & Western States of America
The Slave States of America
Canada, Nova Scotia, New Brunswick, etc.
Tour through Belgium, the Rhine, Switzerland & Holland
Tour in France, Piedmont, Lombardy, the Tyrol & Bavaria

THE BEGINNINGS OF CORNWALL'S TOURIST INDUSTRY

Having established itself as one of Britain's leading holiday regions Cornwall is now year by year attracting more and more tourists from France, Belgium, Holland and Germany. How, why and when did this holiday business begin?

There are no official records of the origins of the county's tourist industry, but contemporary books and articles in journals relate why and when people began coming to Cornwall for other than occupational or business reasons, or out of sheer curiosity.

Annual holidays involving absence from home for one or more weeks are, for the mass of the people, a comparatively recent innovation. Formerly holidays were holy days well spaced out in the religious calendar, as well as local saints' or feast days which were spent merry-making in the parish. Only the rich were able to travel abroad for pleasure, and escape from the English climate.

Many changes in the latter half of the eighteenth century can be attributed to the Industrial Revolution, which had many side effects on our working, domestic and social life. It created amongst other things a thirst for knowledge in many directions, including travel.

Enterprising individuals journeyed, usually on horseback, to places in the British Isles and on the Continent to satisfy their curiosity and their hunger for knowledge. Many of them wrote books, articles and diaries about the places and regions they visited. For instance 1749, 1764, 1770, 1771, 1783 and 1799 are only some of the years in which travel books devoted wholly or partly to Cornwall were published.

The small but growing middle class of industrialists - the new rich - who digested this literature discovered in this way that Cornwall enjoyed the mildest and most equable climate in the British Isles. It was being compared with the south of France and the Canary Islands, and was recommended as suitable for invalids suffering from lung and chest complaints on account of its clean pure air, its warm sea breezes and the almost total absence of snow and frost in the winter and excessive heat in the summer.

Invalids and others who felt they would benefit from the change of air started coming to Cornwall, mainly in the winter. This was towards the end of the eighteenth century. The picturesque fishing villages and small harbours, which are big attractions for the modern tourist, were of no interest to them. Refuse lying about in alleys and narrow streets, the stench of fish and the presence of large numbers of small sailing ships discharging or loading their cargoes - copper ore, heavy blocks of tin, coal, timber, casks of pilchards, crates of hardware and a variety of other merchandise - did not appeal to invalids and semi-invalids. The rough workaday world was unpleasant for people who came for health cures. It was the mild climate and nothing else that attracted people seeking relief from their pulmonary complaints. It was these visitors, mainly consumptives if you like, who unknowingly started something which has since developed into a very large tourist trade.

Penzance was the first place to experience this form of health or medicinal tourism. In another sphere of ailments it was following Matlock, Leamington Spa, Tunbridge Wells, Bath and other inland resorts, but it was destined never to achieve their high reputation as a purely health resort. The Rev. Richard Warner, who toured Cornwall in 1808, wrote that Penzance had already for many years been a resort for invalids from other parts of England. The town soon acquired some renown and became, we are told, a fashionable watering place. The Lysons brothers in volume three of their Magna Britannia, published in 1814, confirmed what Warner had to say, adding that Penzance was much frequented by invalids in the winter. Together with Torquay Penzance was thus breaking new ground in Britain by becoming a seaside health resort. Its remoteness and the lack of a railway there before 1852 meant that only the wealthier invalids could afford a winter holiday, if they could put up with the discomforts of primitive means of transport.

The Gazetteer of the County of Cornwall in 1817 mentioned that hot and cold sea-water baths had been constructed for the use of invalids. The first detailed guide book to the Penzance district - in fact the first in Cornwall - was published in 1815 by a distinguished physician who was resident there from 1813 to 1817 and who was president of the Royal College of Physicians from 1844 to 1856. He was Dr. John Ayrton Paris. His guide book, which ran into three editions, contained information for invalids on the climate of Penzance compared with that of Mediterranean resorts. Another man who helped to publicise Penzance was Edward Collins Giddy, who was born in 1775. He kept records of his own meteorological observations from 1807 to 1827, and published them in the Philosophical Magazine.

Cyrus Redding, a travel author, wrote in 1842 that Penzance was rich in outdoor flowers and shrubs that elsewhere in England were regarded as exotic if grown outside a greenhouse. He was forthright when he wrote that in the churchyard there were numerous tombstones of people who were not local inhabitants, but who had hoped to benefit from the salubrious climate. "Many of these, when medical attendance had become hopeless at home, were sent thither to die" but might have recovered had they been sent earlier.

By the middle of the nineteenth century Penzance had doubled in size. J.S. Courtney in his comprehensive guide book to the district comprising Penzance, St Ives and the Isles of Scilly, whilst warning invalids to consult a physician before deciding to come for a cure suggested that

Penzance might become a summer holiday resort. Then there is a word of apology: "Penzance has ever been more a trading port than a watering place, and hence the inhabitants have not bestowed so much attention on its outward appearance as they would do were it entirely dependent on visitors.... Latterly with a view to increasing their comforts, public promenades and other improvements have been suggested, and one of them, the Esplanade.... is now nearly completed." This was in 1845.

Despite rail connection with Truro in 1852 and with Plymouth and London in 1859 Penzance by the mid-1870's had still not become a greatly frequented summer holiday resort. A guide book of this period reported that "The beach on the western green offers every facility for bathing. The Baths there are good, and the house having been much enlarged and beautified, there is ample accommodation for lodgers under the same roof, where they can enjoy the luxury of sea bathing.... There are now excellent lodgings and lodging houses in almost every part of Penzance.... We notice the establishment of cabs, and we hope the time is not far distant when Bath chairs will be more numerous than they are at present."

The Land's End attracted no attention whatever. It was just one amongst many places around the rugged coast from Mounts Bay to St Ives. Only Lamorna Cove seemed worthy of a day trip. Courtney in 1845 wrote: "Lamorna is usually visited from Penzance on a summer afternoon, and the parties leave the *material* (tea or coffee, currants and sugar) which they have brought with them at one of the cottages, stroll for an hour or two on the sands, or amongst the rocks, and on returning to the cottage they find tea or coffee prepared, with abundance of rich clouted cream, and a heavy cake just ready to be taken from the hearth on which it has been baked."

Flushing, lying across the harbour from Falmouth, had the reputation of being the warmest place in Cornwall in the winter. In the eighteenth century it had achieved some notoriety as the residence of families of many of the officers employed in the Falmouth Post Office Packets which carried the mails to and from Portugal, the West Indies and the United States. It became the centre of a gay social life. In 1790 it was described as a winter resort for invalids, and in 1817 the Gazetteer of the County of Cornwall described it as "a place of considerable resort in the summer season as a watering place." And this was long before Falmouth, much larger but facing east, was thought of as a holiday resort, winter or summer.

The first place in Cornwall to attract holidaymakers on account of its sands and coastal scenery was Bude. Mr. Warner in 1808 wrote that it was to this place that "the many gentry and the invalids from Launceston and other places of the eastern division of the county come to bathe, and breathe the sea air in the summer months." He added that there were "a decent inn and several neat lodging houses" for the accommodation of visitors, but that the resort "not yet having arrived to the refinement of bathing machines, the ladies are put to some little inconvenience in performing the rites of immersion." According to one writer Bude was already a watering place before the opening of the century, but it was not until 1846 that there is any mention of bathing machines.

But opinions differed. Murray's guide of 1850 was not too flattering. It regarded Bude as "a mean watering place of recent origin, consisting of an hotel and some cheerless cottages" but also spoke of "the grand and curious coast.... the vast and picturesque sea-cliffs." A North Cornwall guide of 1889 reported that "Bude has fast grown into notoriety as a bracing north-coast watering place.... Large numbers of health and pleasure seekers visit Bude during the summer months...."

The same guide book mentioned two places close to Bude that were attracting tourists. At St Gennys "several commodious lodging houses have sprung up.... It may be observed that farmhouse lodgings are often the most enjoyable in this particular neighbourhood." Crackington Haven was described as a delightful resort, being a fine example of romantic coastal scenery. Tintagel and Boscastle, now so popular with tourists, do not get a mention in this 1889 guide to North Cornwall.

As a holiday resort Newquay is of much more recent growth than either Penzance or Bude. Davies Gilbert, Warner and Murray did not mention it although they went close to it. All that Cyrus Redding had to say in 1842 was that "St Columb Minor has an inlet with a quay and a shelter for small vessels, called Newquay, where a considerable fishery is carried on." It was then a small fishing village of thatched cottages with a population of less than 300.

Newquay harbour changed hands in 1838, and the quays were extended to handle growing shipments of minerals mined a few miles in the interior. Rapidly increasing trade brought more people to the place. Nature had provided the basic ingredients - beaches and coastal scenery - for a holiday resort, and only a passenger-carrying railway was needed to complement them. But already in 1847, some thirty years before the arrival of the first passenger train, Newquay was being frequented for bathing.

The period of rapid expansion began only in 1876, and by the end of the century the town had become Cornwall's leading resort with the largest hotel in the county opened there in 1890. An author writing in a Cornish journal in 1898 made some scathing comments about the lack of inspiration and total absence of town planning during this period of rapid growth. He deplored that the main street was built too narrow and with dangerous curves, and felt that it did not come up to the town's pretension to be the first of Cornish watering places.

Just as bad was the lack of a promenade between the houses and the cliffs; it would have made the town far more attractive. He goes on: "Perhaps when the importance of the matter is fully realised care will be taken to safeguard the future in regard to ground outside the town which the builder has not yet invaded."

F.W.L. Stockdale who wrote of his excursion into Cornwall in 1824, discovered Perran Porth, a few miles down the coast south-west of Newquay. It was, he said, "much resorted to during the bathing season on account of its fine sandy beach and healthy situation." Since Redding and Murray passed it by it could not have been well known. As Bude was to Launceston so Perranporth was to Truro, some of whose inhabitants no doubt wanted to be in the swim.

Of still more recent growth than Newquay as holiday resorts are St Ives, Looe and Fowey. During the nineteenth century they were places of much activity, preoccupied with fishing, boat and ship-building and seaborne trade. These activities did not easily fit in with the sedate atmosphere of Georgian and Victorian holidays. It was only when their industries and commerce began to decline - although that took a long time - that these places turned their attention to the holiday business. And for this they were superbly equipped by Nature with magnificent coastal or river scenery. Their narrow and picturesque streets retain the best from the past when they were dirty and untidy places.

Both the Redding and Murray guide books dismissed St Ives as a town suitable as a resort, the former depicting it as "but a populous fishing place, with two or three mines in the vicinity." It was left to Courtney in 1845 to look beyond the immediate present. Writing of the terrace of houses and the new road above Porthminster beach he commented: "Beneath it is a beautiful gently-sloping beach composed of the the finest shell sand, untainted with mud, and unmixed with pebbles or gravel of any kind.... It is a delightful bathing place, equalled by very few in England; and nothing is wanting to make it a fashionable one but a little enterprise on the part of the inhabitants, to induce them to erect public baths and good lodging houses on the shore for the reception and use of visitors, who have already evinced an eagerness to procure such accommodation."

But he was less enthusiastic about the workaday St Ives down at the bottom of the hill: "A walk from the terrace to the 'island' would present little else but cause for disappointment to the traveller, who had formed his estimate of the place from the view he had on his approach to it."

A handbook of the mid-1870's described St Ives as "a quaint old fishing town with irregular and narrow streets.... The spirit of improvement, however, is beginning to creep into it. Within the last few years some good houses have been built on the various terraces overlooking Porthminster Cove and the Bay.... The beaches are remarkably clean and beautiful.... A little enterprise, capital and taste seem to be all that are wanting here to found another Torquay or Brighton in the far west."

Walter White, librarian to the Royal Society, in his book "A Londoner's Walk to the Land's End," published in 1855, was in too much

102

of a hurry to do more than take a glance at St Ives. He went by train from Marazion to St Ives Road station (now St Erth) and recommended his readers to "Go by rail.... and if you wish to have a chat with fishwomen who are carrying basketfuls of their scaly merchandise from one port to another, take a third-class ticket, and you will come to some conclusions respecting human nature under one of its sturdy aspects." Then he suggests walking with them the two or three miles "till you come to the top of the ascent which commands St Ives, and there, while they trudge onwards, sit down and look at what is before you. Not a handsome town.... quite the reverse.... Travellers to the Mediterranean say that it reminds them of towns on the shores of Greece: unrestrained and picturesque.... Do not disenchant yourself by going down into the town, but strike off the nearest way along the cliffs...."

A Cornish diarist in 1842 entered a brief note in his diary stating that Fowey was the Montpellier of England. In what respect he did not say, but we know what he meant. Murray in 1850 condescended to mention without excessive enthusiasm that a trip by water up the river to Lostwithiel past the well-wooded slopes "is a favourite excursion." He had nothing else to say apart from a lengthy re-hash of second-hand Fowey history.

This old seaport was very slow to gain recognition as a holiday resort. A guide published in 1892 drew attention to a booklet written ten years previously and entitled "An Unknown Watering Place," which aroused some interest in the town. The guide also quoted in full a long letter written by 'Q' in December 1889 to the Morning Post newspaper extolling the mild winters that Fowey could offer invalids whose ailments they hoped to cure by going to foreign resorts.

The same guide book criticised modern ideas of improvement which were depriving the streets of their picturesque appearance with the removal of quaint old buildings and two archways across the streets. One archway at the Bodinnick ferry slipway was demolished and an inn nearby was replaced by a modern hotel. The guide book pointed out that bathing facilities at Fowey were restricted, and recommended visitors to betake themselves by boat across the river to one or another of the small creeks on the opposite shore of the estuary. The lack of good beaches was however compensated by some magnificent riverside scenery upstream in the direction of Lerryn and Lostwithiel.

Mevagissey was out of favour with travellers in the nineteenth century who put their ideas in writing. The Murray guide for 1850 described this very busy commercial fishery centre as "noted for dirt and pilchards." The writer should have added that Mevagissey built its own fishing luggers and carried on an active export trade in pilchards to Italy. Of Padstow the same observer wrote that it was "one of those antiquated unsavoury fishing towns which are viewed most agreeably from a distance." He could have added, but did not, that this unsavoury place had five shipyards turning out ocean-going schooners, as well as fishing boats. And it also had an active import and export trade.

Times have changed, and both Mevagissey and Padstow have been taken over by the motorised summer day-tripper. Neither place has much to offer in the way of bathing beaches and were therefore never to become watering places. Across the Camel estuary from Padstow is Rock, which was described in the North Cornwall guide in 1889 as a very attractive watering place. "In addition to its neat hotel and a few very pretty lodging houses which are well patronised in the season, a gentleman, resident in America, who owes his birth to Rock, has had erected several handsome villa residences, with a promise to extend their number if his speculation answers."

Falmouth was not one of the early holiday resorts. Although a Falmouth guide was published in 1815 it was specifically written for the benefit of travellers passing through the port, which handled much passenger traffic. It contained "directions to the public offices, lodging houses, inns, taverns, etc.... being a complete directory to strangers going abroad in the packets."

It was not until the coming of the railway in 1863 that Falmouth seriously went into the holiday business. It suddenly realised that it was the most southerly town in the British Isles, and possessed all the topographical assets and the makings of a fine holiday resort, and set about drawing full advantage from them. It could claim to be a winter as well as a summer resort when the more sheltered southerly fringe of the town was developed.

The Handbook of Cornwall, published in the mid-1870's, commented that in the districts of Grove Hill and Gyllingdune "the invalid may sit sheltered from wind and cold, comforted in early spring by a warm genial temperature from a whole day's sun, and cheered from infirmity and pain by the life and beauty of the surrounding scene.... Within the last four or five years the southern part of Falmouth has been so much altered and improved by the new roads and drives opened up by the Earl of Kimberley, that persons who have been absent for that period would almost fail to recognise it...."

A CORNISH DIARIST AND ESTATE STEWARD

The diaries of William Pease are well known to a few people, in particular to those who have used them for research into aspects of Cornish history. However, very little has been written about the man himself, or about the literary value of the second series of his diaries that run in unbroken sequence from 1850 to 1881.

Wider recognition of Pease as a diarist is long overdue, for his work is a valuable contribution to Westcountry literature, first as a unique record of estate management in the Victorian era and, second, for his prose, which is of a very high and consistent standard throughout the thirty-two years.

Very little is known as yet of his forebears. His father, also William, was a native of Lanteglos-by-Fowey, and may have been a member of the Pease family who farmed Lawhibbet, in that parish. His mother was Ann Harris, of yeoman stock, whose family lived at the hamlet of Treskilling, near Luxulyan. They were married at Tywardreath Church in December 1807.

Their only son, William, our diarist, was born on Christmas Day 1808. He died in 1881. His life thus spanned the period of greatest changes this country had ever known. He was born into a world without railways, and left it with the railway network practically complete. He saw many radical changes in the country's social, economic and industrial life. Yet the immense upheavals that took place in his lifetime are not reflected to any great extent in the diaries. And only two new inventions are casually noted: photography and electric lighting. The diaries contain a day-by-day record of his occupational activities, adding up to the story of the last thirty-two years of his life. If changes in the outside world affected him he treated them as merely incidental.

As in most diaries, there are occasional brief gaps, and in the case of Pease it is clear that gaps only mean avoiding repetition; therefore what he did not write down on blank days is not missed. He is revealed as an outstanding character with a single-minded devotion to work, to the highest moral principles and to Christian ideals such as these were interpreted by the Victorians.

He was brought up by his grandmother at Treskilling, a settlement in a bleak environment of barren moors and granite outcrops. He lived here from the age of three until he was eight. They then removed to Tywardreath, a small agricultural village that within a few years was to become a bustling and over-crowded mining township. William's mother had died when he and his only sister, younger than he, were still in their infancy. She was interred in Luxulyan churchyard.

William had no brothers. His sister died of an incurable but un-

105

named illness when still quite young. It was not his father but William himself who, at the age of twenty-three, sent his sister to Plymouth to consult a specialist. The latter's subsequent report was that there was no hope for her. Late at night on July 16, 1832, William wrote in his diary: "At eleven o'clock this evening my dear sister desired that W. Rundle should make her coffin, which is to be of double deal & painted white, and that he should have a Hat Band also the Minister & Clarke - her bearers who she has chosen to have white Gloves. She desires to be buried near Grandmother & to have another such tomb."

Near her grandmother; not her mother, whom she had scarcely known. She lingered on for another six weeks, and when dying on August 28, she said she was happy. She was interred on September 2. William was so stricken with grief at his sister's death that he made no further entries in his diary for that year, 1832.

William and his sister were virtually orphans. There is no mention anywhere in the diaries of their relations with their father. He is accorded only two brief mentions about twenty years after William's sister had died. One is forced to the conclusion that their father was not living with them during the period prior to her death. It was an aunt who looked after her.

It is not known for what profession or career young William Pease was trained, or where he went to school. He was not born to privilege or wealth. It is certain that self-education had much to do with the acquisition of the vast fund of knowledge that enabled him to master without fuss many problems and awkward situations he encountered all through his life. He was always jotting down the titles of books, and one can only assume they were works he intended acquiring for his own use. Books on engineering, agriculture and farming, chemistry, law, Nature, mathematics, the care of animals, religion, geology, philosphy, astronomy, geography, science, education, languages, the arts, well-known classics.... there is no end to the range of reading matter.

In May 1837 William married Caroline, one of the daughters of William Cossentine, who farmed Manelly in St Veep parish, overlooking the River Fowey nearly opposite Golant. They had four children. A daughter, Anne, born in 1838, and a son, William, in 1840, survived them. The other two were girls, born in 1842 and 1844. They were both given the same baptismal names - Caroline Cossentine - and both died as infants.

Growing up without a mother, losing his only sister, and then two of his own children dying in infancy, probably had a deep effect on William Pease. These personal tragedies many have accounted for the compassion he often showed towards others.

The first series of diaries running from 1832 to 1849 reveal that he combined the functions of a surveyor, a salesman, business administrator and manager. Later he is seen also as an accomplished legal man and as a sound and astute negotiator. From 1832 onwards he was working for

Joseph Thomas Treffry of Fowey, first as clerk and then as his agent - a kind of general manager - at Par.

He was closely involved with the commercial, financial and general engineering aspects of Treffry's smelting, granite quarrying, china clay, shipping and other interests in the Par area. They included the cutting of a canal, the construction of Par Harbour and of the huge granite viaduct in the Luxulyan Valley, the laying down of several short railroads and the extraction of silver from lead ore at the Par Smelting Works.

Pease remained in Mr. Treffry's service until the latter died in January 1850. Hitherto his diaries served as a business man's notebooks and aide-memoires. They are full of mathematical calculations, prices, estimates of costs, notes on shipments of copper ore and granite, imports of coal, freight rates, measurements of new sailing ships to be built at Fowey, technical details of canal, bridge and railroad construction, and scribbled notes on matters discussed at meetings and with all manner of people involved in or with the Treffry industrial complex.

They are not diaries in the literary sense, but they contain much useful material for the very localised history of the industries created and developed by the man who was Cornwall's largest employer of labour in the 1830's and 1840's.

On Mr. Treffry's death William Pease was offered, and accepted, the stewardship of the Cornish estates of Lady Grenville, of Dropmore in Buckinghamshire. This move into a totally different world brought heavy responsibilities calling for the exercise of a powerful, mature and thoroughly well equipped intellect.

Lady Grenville, born Ann Pitt, was a cousin of the younger William Pitt; sister of the second Lord Camelford of Boconnoc, in Cornwall; and widow of William Wyndham Grenville, who had served as a member of William Pitt's cabinet, and who had died in 1834.

The Grenville estates in Cornwall comprised well over fifty farms and other properties, including mines and china clay deposits, all administered from the stewardry at Boconnoc.

The complexities of estate management on this scale are very apparent as one follows the almost daily journeys on horseback or by gig or dog cart; the meetings - sometimes up to a dozen in a single day - with all types of people; the investigation of complaints and disputes; the tours of inspection; the surveying of land; the valuation of crops and livestock; the holding of rent courts and tithe audits; the regular attendance at courts of justice; negotiating the sale or purchase of land and other property, and so on.

Pease was also vice-chairman of the Highway Board and surveyor of the county bridges in the Eastern Division of Cornwall. This office included amongst its responsibilities the periodical inspection of all sixty-five bridges under his charge. He planned and supervised the construction of the present bridge linking East and West Looe, and the replacement of the cutwaters and abutments of the bridge at Wadebridge.

Pease's stewardship was so successful that four years later, in 1854, he was given the additional responsibility of managing Lady Grenville's extensive properties in Buckinghamshire. This involved at least four, and usually many more, visits a year to Dropmore and London.

His work became still more varied. We may find him spending a whole week travelling about the rough stony Cornish lanes on horseback or by gig in very primitive conditions and spending his nights at farm houses, cottages or inns, and a day or two later in London meeting City bankers and legal experts about leases, mortgages, taxation, legacies, lawsuits and similar matters.

Often when in London he fitted in visits to museums, exhibitions, picture galleries, theatres and famous buildings, including the new wonder of the age - the Crystal Palace. On Sundays he attended, and often commented on, church services. On one occasion he witnessed a Commons debate in which both Gladstone and Disraeli took part. And when we read that he sometimes travelled by the new underground railway we realise that even in his time there were already traffic problems in London's crowded streets.

Similarly his very occasional holiday trips to Scotland, Wales, France, Belgium and Switzerland with one or another member of his family or with a friend, are written up in considerable detail.

Although he spent nearly half his time away from home our diarist was very much a family man. He brought his family up to be outward-looking and unparochial. They kept open house at Boconnoc for their many friends and relatives, and were continually entertaining, sometimes providing overnight accommodation for their guests. The family attended church regularly, and William himself, when not absent from home, often took a Sunday School class.

Unlike some diarists, William Pease wrote neither for pleasure nor for posterity, but in support of a disciplined and orderly mind packed with knowledge and facts. He lived for his work, and did not waste time on futile pleasures. His life was so full, and his contacts and discussions with people of all types and professions so numerous that he just had to make day-to-day notes for ready and future reference.

The diaries are written up in consistently simple and precise English without a single superfluous word among the 300,000 odd they contain. Clarity, directness and simplicity are the secret of his strong and impressive prose. He sticks to facts without any embellishments, and being a man of great integrity and discretion he avoids expressing opinions and emotions, or drawing comparisons. And if he is very occasionally critical of anyone it is only to justify the course of action he was obliged to take.

While he exercised scrupulous fairness and unyielding firmness in his business dealings and private affairs, he was capable of forgiveness and compassion. A classic example of his treatment of those who broke the accepted code of morals was his dismissal of his clerk who had become the father of a child born to an unmarried village girl. To Pease this was a forgivable sin. He was instrumental in finding the dismissed man another job, which happened to be in the Home Counties, near London, and from time to time during his visits to Dropmore Pease made a point of spending an evening with him or to have a meal with him.

By the nature of his work there was purpose behind all he did. Therefore, since the diaries are a record of his work it is often necessary to analyse what he writes, or read between the lines. His wife's many relatives and his own family connections, other than his father, are frequently found in the diaries when social visits, sickness and deaths are noted in simple factual terms, but without comment, sentimental or otherwise.

William Pease was widely known and greatly esteemed. As an estate steward he established an enviable reputation, and several owners of large properties in the South and South-West of England consulted him for his advice on the management of their estates, or on the value of their land or houses.

NOTES

1. *Victoria County History, Part V Romano-British Cornwall.* 1924.
2. A.G. Langdon, *Victoria County History, Early Christian Monuments.* 1906. Opinions expressed in the text about a few of these inscribed stones are the author's and are purely speculative. The period in which the stones are believed to have been erected seems to be isolated and unrelated to the periods immediately preceding and following it. It is probably the least documented, archaeologically, of the recognised periods in Cornwall's history.
3. Rev. F.C. Hingeston-Randolph, editor, *Register of Bishop Grandisson,* 1894. This letter of Grandisson is significant since it explains why the lives of the Welsh, Irish and Breton saints who came to Cornwall have been relegated to the realms of legend and fancy. It is incredible that no church in Cornwall or Devon has preserved in its chest the record of the life of its local patron saint, assuming of course that the bishop's directive was heeded.
4. R. Doehaerd, *L'Expansion Economique Belge au Moyen Age.* 1946. There is, so far, no authentic evidence of shipments of tin from Cornwall or Devon to the Continent, direct or via London, in the post-Roman pre-Norman period. However, the virtually uninterrupted tradition of Belgian metal-working means that supplies were obtained. These could only have come from the already existing source.
5. Germain Bapst, *L'Etain.* 1884. This French historian gives in his book what is probably the most complete account ever written of the vast range of products and articles made of tin or incorporating it, from the earliest uses down to its applications in the late Middle Ages. Although Bapst is not concerned with the commerce in tin his work implies that it must have been extensive and enduring. Only a selection of the metal's manifold uses are mentioned in this essay.
6. Germain Bapst, *L'Etain.* 1884.
7. *The Great Rolls of the Pipe, 7-9 Ric. I and I John.*
8. *The Calendar of Close Rolls, 6 Edward II.*
9. *The Clendar of Patent Rolls, 21 Edward III.*
10. A Schaube, *Handelsgeschichte der Romanischen Voelker des Mittelmeergebietes bis zum Ende der Kreuzzuege.* 1906. Schaube is only one of many continental historians who have noticed and reported the existence of the international trade in Cornwall's tin in the Middle Ages. In his book he gives us glimpses of its Mediterranean ramifications, whilst the Italian Francesco Pegolotti, a prominent member of the Bardi Society in the 14th century, takes us further afield to the starting points of the penetration of the trade by Italian mercantile companies into distant Asia.
11. Schaube A. *Handelsgeschichte, etc.*
12. Francesco Pegolotti, *La Pratica della Mercatura,* editior Allen Evans, Medieval Academy of America. 1936.
13. Francesco Pegolotti, *La Pratica della Mercatura, etc.*
14. H.B. Walters, *The Church Bells of England.* 1912.
15. *The Calendar of Liberate Rolls, 31-36 Henry III.* Restriction of space prevents a more detailed and broader selection of purchases of tin by the Crown for specific applications. Acquisitions of the metal for use in such government works as building and bell-founding continued all through the Middle Ages.
16. The Calendar of Liberate Rolls, 32-46 Henry III.
17. Charles Welch, *History of the Worshipful Company of Pewterers,* 1912.
18. Germain Bapst, *L'Etain.* 1884.
19. Germain Bapst, *L'Etain.* 1884.
20. Jules Balasque, *Etudes Historiques sur la Ville de Bayonne.* 1862.
21. Jules Balasque, *Etudes Historiques, etc.*
22. *Ministers' Accounts, Duchy of Cornwall, 14th century.*
23. *Register of Edward the Black Prince, folio 124.* HMSO 1931.
24. P. Studer, editor *The Port Books of Southampton 1427-30.* 1913.

111

25. L.M. Midgley, *Ministers' Accounts, Earldom of Cornwall 1296-7*. 1945.
26. L.M. Midgley, *Ministers' Accounts, etc.*
27. Maurice Beresford, *New Towns of the Middle Ages*. 1967.
28. T.F. Tout, *Chapters in the Administrative History of Medieval England, vol. 5*. 1930.
29. G. Concanen, *Ministers' Accounts, Duchy of Cornwall, 1349*, cited in the Trial at Bar Rowe v. Brenton. 1830.
30. Rev. F.C. Hingeston-Randolph, editor *Register of Bishop Grandisson*. 1894.
31. *Ministers' Accounts, Duchy of Cornwall, Rolls No. 6 & 7, SC 6 816-823*. These annual Ministers' accounts reveal that the adverse effects of the Black Death were felt until the end of the 14th century and beyond. They also show that the subsequent plague of 1361 caused the complete cessation of commercial fishing at five traditional fishery porths on the coast of West Penwith.
32. *Register of Edward the Black Prince, folio 100*. HMSO 1931.
33. Matthias Dunn, *The Migrations and Habits of the Pilchard*, a lecture delivered at the Fisheries Exhibition, Truro, in 1895.
34. *Victoria County History, The Fisheries*, 1906.
35. *Parliamentary Papers, vol. xi, 1857*. Report of House of Commons Select Committee on the Rating of Mines.
36. This essay is the author's severely condensed account of James Silk Buckingham's Autobiography that was published in two volumes and covered his life up to the age of twenty-nine years. He died as soon as this first part of his account of his travels and adventures was published. He was unable to commit to paper the story of the rest of his life.
37. Boase & Courtenay, *Biblioteca Cornubiensis, vols. I & II*. 1874 & 1882.

Other titles available from

DYLLANSOW TRURAN

CORNISH BEDSIDE BOOK NO.1.
John Keast

Place-names, customs, dialects, remedies and recipes are nicely balanced by short essays and stories by early travellers, historical events and extracts from diaries. A throughly entertaining book.

Card Covers 9506431 8 1

VISITORS TO CORNWALL
Ida Procter

As J.C. Trewin says in his Introduction- 'Ida Procter can recreate her guests most surely... Everyone is here; Francis Kilvert for example, Ceila Fiennes is here - at St. Austell. Nearly two centuries later the young Beatrix Potter was arriving by train at Falmouth.
It is an enchanting book.'

Paperback 0 907566 27 8
Hardback 0 907566 26 X

HOW LONG IS FOREVER *Memories of a Cornish Maid*
Ethelwyn Watts

Born in the changing years of the decade that followed the First World War, the author describes her home parish as 'perhaps the most Cornish part of Cornwall' and she paints a word picture of a magical land.

Card Covers 0 907566 30 8
Hardback 0 907566 89 8

THE BOUNCING HILLS *Dialect Tales and Light Verse*
Jack Clemo

Jack Clemo says 'I contributed many dialect tales to Cornish Almanacks before the war capturing the lighter side of Clay country village life as it was 50 years ago. I have chosen eight of these stories, and have added a selection of my comic verse (not in dialect, but with a Cornish flavour). There are about 20 short poems, mostly written for or about children'
This is a book from a Cornish literary giant shedding a new light on Cornwall's own blind poet.

Card Covers 0 907566 38 3
Hard Covers 0 907566 39 1

THE HISTORY OF FALMOUTH
Dr. James Whetter

The author's considerable knowledge of life in the 17th Century Cornwall provides much new information about the origins of the old town - its growth over three and a half centuries and its social, cultural and religious history.

Hard Covers 0 907566 01 4
Card covers 0 907566 02 2

THE KING OF MID-CORNWALL

The Life of Joseph Thomas Treffry
John Keast

Joseph Thomas Treffry (1792-1890) has been aptly described as 'A captain of industry, master of his own economic fate, an assertive individualist soul who pioneered in the development of transportation to facilitate the exploitation of his mines and the marketing of the ores they produced!

Paper Back 0 907566 29 4
Hard Back 0 907566 19 7

STATELY HOMES IN AND AROUND TRURO

Rex Barratt

His book misses nothing of the gems of a favoured area - from ancient Polwhele and Killagordon (to which film star Kathleen Hepburn was a frequent visitor) to Tullimar - where Kilvert, of diary fame, spent a holiday in 1870.

Card Covers 9506431 6 5

ST. IVES HERITAGE

Lena & Donald Bray

Recollections and records of St. Ives, Carbis Bay and Lelant.
'This patient, well researched and loving look at the history, customs and general lifestyle of this jewel of the North Cornish Coast makes this an unusually endearing narrative' WESTERN MORNING NEWS.

Hard Covers 0 907566 07 3
Card Covers 0 907566 08 1

JOHN KNILL - HIS LIFE AND TIMES

Beryl James

'John Knill, Mayor of St. Ives, customs official and adventurer extraordinary, was a remarkable son of the rumbustious 18th century... The life-style of this lawyer-cum-pursuer of smugglers makes a scenario fit for any Holywood epic.

Card Covers 0 907566 06 5

CORNISH SAYINGS, SUPERSTITIONS AND REMEDIES

Kathleen Hawke

'What makes all Mrs. Hawke's work on dialect particularly interesting is that she has lived for many years in both mid-Cornwall and west-Cornwall' K.C. PHILLIPS.

0 907566 04 9

CORNISH QUIZ

R.S. Best

Over 500 questions and answers on Cornwall and things Cornish. Illustrated by C.M. Pellowe.

9506431 4 9

MEMORIES OF A TRURONIAN IN WAR AND PEACE

Rex Barratt

The picture of the city that emerges, how it adapted its ways of life to war, the excitement of Royal Visits, life in church and school, politics, music and drama, shopkeepers and local characters, are all faithfully recorded and illustrated.

Card Covers 0 907566 00 6